TIME RANGERS

8. A Fate Worse Than Death

"It's a German bomber!" he yelled. "Get down!"

She laughed. "Don't be silly. We don't have Germans on our farm."

Alice could see the panic in his eyes as he approached and she screamed. Jacko reached her at full speed, almost knocking her over, but he managed to grab her with both arms. He lifted her up off her feet and kept on running, sending the apples and the football flying into the air.

"Oh God, I've left it too late," he cried, finding Alice heavier than he expected. "I'm not gonna make it in time. . ."

Join the Time Rangers on tour!

TIME RANGERS

8. A Fate Worse Than Death

Rob Childs

Hippo

DAZZA
GOALKEEPER – 1

WORM
RIGHT-BACK – 2

STOPPER
CENTRE-BACK – 5

RAKESH
RIGHT-MIDFIELD – 4

MR STOPPARD
MANAGER

JACKO
CENTRE-MIDFIELD – 8

SPEEDIE
RIGHT-WINGER – 7

RYAN
CENTRE-FORWARD – 9

ANIL
LEFT-WINGER – 11

MR THOMAS
MANAGER

For my wife Joy, with special thanks

Scholastic Children's Books,
Commonwealth House,
1–19 New Oxford Street,
London WC1A 1NU, UK
a division of Scholastic Ltd
London ~ New York ~ Toronto ~ Sydney ~ Auckland
Mexico City ~ New Delhi ~ Hong Kong

First published in the UK by Scholastic Ltd, 1998

Typeset by M Rules
Printed by Cox and Wyman Ltd, Reading, Berks.

10 9 8 7 6 5 4 3 2 1

1 Underground

"Aaaghh! An alien!"

Ryan staggered back in mock horror and collided with Jacko.

"Watch it!" came the protest. "It's only Worm in a gas mask."

"Phew!" Ryan grinned. "Quick, take it off, Worm, it's horrible."

"Very funny. I already have done."

"Have you? Better put it back on, then, I reckon."

Worm scowled and replaced the gas mask in its cardboard box. "Fancy having to carry a thing like that around with you during the war."

"My gran's still got hers in the loft back at the farm," Jacko said. "It's almost as good as new. Never been worn."

He glanced at his watch, impatient for the football action to restart. Jacko was captain of Tanfield Rangers Under-13s squad that were in London to take part in a weekend soccer tournament, the September Sixes.

This was the second day, but the teams were spending the Sunday morning touring a World War II exhibition staged at St Pancras railway station. The displays also spread along the corridors of the Tube station below and the Rangers had worked their way deep underground.

Worm was in his element. He had sampled rationed foodstuffs like dried eggs, tried on an army uniform, handled weapons and sat in the cockpit of a model Spitfire fighter plane. He was now engrossed in studying a set of photographs showing the flattened houses in bombed London streets.

"The bombing raids went on for months in the Blitz, you know," he said to anyone who might have been listening. "People took shelter down here in the Tube every night. They slept on bunk beds and had sing-songs to keep up their spirits. I've read all about it."

"Surprise, surprise," scoffed Dazza, the Rangers goalkeeper. "You're like a walking encyclopedia when it comes to history."

"Yeah, and just as boring," added his pal, Rakesh.

"This isn't boring," Worm enthused. "I mean, look at these shots of evacuees waiting to board a train. Poor kids. Bet they've got no idea where they're going or if they'll ever see their parents again."

"Better than staying in the city and

getting bombed," said Dazza. "It was much safer in the countryside."

"You try telling my gran that," Jacko chuckled. "She nearly got killed by a stray bomb that fell on our farm."

"Really?" said Worm. "What happened?"

"It's a long story," he answered, yawning. "Gran often goes on about it. You'll have to meet her sometime. Some evacuee saved her life."

"I didn't know that," Worm said, all agog with interest.

"At last! Something Worm doesn't know about history," Ryan laughed and then aimed a kick at the football he had in a carrier bag. It sent the bag spinning out of his grasp, almost landing on a plate of dried eggs.

"Give that to me," demanded his dad, one of the team's managers. He'd already taken the ball off Ryan once for dribbling it along the platform. "You're a menace with that thing. I don't know

why you brought it here."

Mr Thomas realized it was a silly thing to say. He could barely remember taking his son anywhere without a ball for company as well.

As Ryan employed his usual delaying tactics, a man called out to them.

"Any of you lads want to dress up and have your photo taken? See what you look like in the kind of clothes kids wore in those days."

Ryan stared at the collection of short trousers, woolly cardigans and sleeveless pullovers. "Huh! I'd look a complete prat!" he snorted.

"Sounds perfect," smirked his dad. "We'd all like a good laugh. Go and get changed, Ryan."

"No way! I wouldn't be seen dead in that old clobber."

"I'm sure that can be arranged too," said the manager darkly. "Right, I want two more volunteers. You and you will do – and no arguing."

The photographer led Ryan, Jacko and Worm behind a screen to change. The teasing from their teammates was nothing compared to what greeted their reappearance ten minutes later.

The embarrassed trio stood sheepishly together in long grey, ill-fitting shorts held up by uncomfortable pairs of braces. Gas mask boxes dangled from their shoulders and name tags were strung around their necks. Each carried an empty suitcase by his side, although Ryan still clung on to the football bag.

"Get a load of these refugees!" cackled Rakesh.

"Evacuees, not refugees, you idiot," grinned Dazza. "Mind you, I think you could be right. Who'd want to give a home to this scruffy lot?"

"Any more jokes and I'll give you another black eye," snarled Ryan.

The goalkeeper automatically put a hand to his eye, a mysterious wound picked up somehow during the previous day's soccer action. "At least I'd have a matching pair then," he laughed.

"You'd look like a giant panda!" Rakesh teased him.

"Better than being like Just William and his gang here."

"Right, that does it!" yelled Ryan. "C'mon, let's get him."

It was just as well that Dazza was quick off the mark. He was always ready to dash off his line to win a race for the ball against an attacker. Now he put that practice to good use, sprinting along the corridor and up some stairs, pursued by the short-trousered gang.

"Oi! Come back here," shouted the photographer. "You can't go off in those clothes."

Too late. They'd gone. The last he saw of the disappearing figures were the suitcases being waved wildly over their heads as they clattered up the stairs in their scuffed black shoes.

"Don't worry," Mr Thomas reassured him. "They won't go far."

Little did he know just how wrong he could be. The manager of Tanfield Rangers had no idea that the initials TR on the players' shirts might well stand instead for *Time Rangers*.

2 Vanishing act

"Where did he go?"

"Dunno."

"This way – I think."

The three chasers stampeded round a corner and found themselves at the foot of a long escalator.

"He must've gone up there," panted Jacko.

"Can't see him," said Worm, gazing the length of the moving staircase.

"I can!" exclaimed Ryan, pointing. "Look, there he is. C'mon, after him. Don't let him escape."

The escalator was too slow for their

liking and they began to jog up the steps, squirming past other people.

"Hey! Just William!" came a shout. "You're going the wrong way."

They whirled round to see Dazza travelling in the opposite direction on the "down" escalator.

"He's doubled back on us," cried Jacko.

Dazza pulled faces at them as he passed by. "Can't catch me!"

"We'll see about that!" muttered Ryan, bashing somebody on the knee with his suitcase as he turned and started to head back down.

His gang reluctantly followed, struggling against the escalator's upwards motion and the tide of irritated passengers. Dazza glanced over his shoulder and panicked as he saw what they were doing.

"We're gonna get you, Dazza. . ." he heard Ryan's loud threat echoing off the walls, ". . . *gonna get yooouuu. . .*"

Dazza broke into a clumsy run then checked back to see how close they were. He did a double-take. They'd totally disappeared from view.

"Must've ducked down out of sight, trying to fool me."

As he neared the bottom of the escalator, he jumped the final few steps and was about to dash off when a nasty thought crossed his mind.

"Oh, no! Surely not," he gasped. "Not again."

He risked a quick peek up the escalator his teammates had been on, still half-expecting to see them crouched below the handrail. But nobody was there. Dazza closed his eyes and leaned against the wall.

"Vanished. Just like that," he murmured. "And bet I don't need three guesses where they've gone to either."

He waited for a minute, hoping they might somehow reappear, then heaved a sigh. "Now what am I supposed to go and tell the managers?"

"And just what do you think you three are doing?" shrilled a plump old lady in front of them. "Playing silly games on the escalator is not allowed."

"Especially at a time like this," added her friend. "You ought to be ashamed of yourselves."

Their path was completely blocked. The footballers had no option but to let the escalator carry them upwards again on its rickety journey.

"I don't know where you boys suddenly came from, charging down on us like that," continued the plump one. "You gave me quite a turn."

"Well, are you going to apologize for giving us a fright?" demanded the other. "Where are your manners?"

"Sorry," they mumbled, heads down.

"Pardon? Speak up."

"Sorry," they repeated in chorus, louder.

"That's better. And I hope you *are* sorry too." She eyed them suspiciously, peering at the labels around their necks. "I trust that you were not trying to run away."

Ryan made a furtive little wiggle with his finger against his temple to indicate he thought the two women were both batty. Worm wasn't so sure. As they rode higher, he stared at the advertising posters on the wall with increasing alarm.

Even when they reached the top there was no escaping the attentions of their self-appointed escorts. Ryan and Jacko were stopped in their tracks as they made for the other escalator.

"And where do you think you're going now?" the plump one shrilled.

"Back down. Why? What's it to you?" stated Ryan rudely.

"You insolent boy," she snapped. "You need a good hiding."

"Having some trouble, ladies?" enquired a ticket collector.

"Yes, it's these cheeky blighters," she complained. "I believe they're trying to slip back home."

"Are they now?" he said sternly. "And I don't suppose they intend paying their fare either. Can I see your tickets, gentlemen?"

Jacko sighed. "Look, there's been a bit of a misunderstanding, that's all,"

he began. "We've just got separated from the rest of our party."

"You have indeed," the man said. "Follow me and I'll make sure you find them again. Can't have you getting lost, can we?"

He indicated the way towards the mainline station but they refused to go. Ryan said something he shouldn't.

"None of your lip either, lad. I'll give you a clip round the ear."

"You can't do that!" Ryan said defiantly. "I'll report you. It's against the law."

"Oh, is it now?" The man gave a hollow laugh. "Since when? The law will box your ears as well if a bobby gets his hands on you."

Worm tugged at Jacko's sleeve. "Er . . . I hate to say this, but I think we're out of time again. I've just twigged what's going on here."

"What d'yer mean?" Jacko hissed.

"Well, look around you. Everywhere's sort of different – y'know, old fashioned, like. Get a load of this guy's uniform for a start."

"Oh, brilliant!" Jacko groaned. "Now where have we ended up?"

The ticket collector answered the question for him. "Right, come with me before I really lose my temper. Got better things to do than waste my time on you lot. Don't you know there's a war on?"

3 Homeward bound

"No pushing, please, dearies," called out a woman with a clipboard. "Keep in line now. Plenty of seats for everyone on the train."

Worm, Jacko and Ryan stood in the queue of children with cases and bags. There were dozens, maybe hundreds of them, on the station platform, all looking pale and bewildered. Some of the younger ones were in tears.

"This is ridiculous," Ryan fumed. "What are we doing here? Let's just make a run for it. They'd never catch us."

"Want a bet?" said Jacko. "I saw that

ticket bloke speak to those two coppers over there by the wall. He probably told them to keep an eye on us troublemakers."

"First time I've ever been on a steam train," said Worm.

Ryan stared at him. "You make it sound as if you're actually looking forward to it. This is no time to take up train-spotting as a hobby."

The woman walked down the line of evacuees, checking names on labels against those on her clipboard. She stopped by the travellers.

"Oh, you're big boys, aren't you? Where do you come from?"

There was no point in telling the truth. "Our streets were bombed last night so we've been sent here," Worm answered, acting upset.

"Oh, you poor darlings," she clucked. "I do hope your families are safe and well."

Receiving no response, she thought it better not to pry any further and studied their labels instead. "Oh dear, somebody's just written nicknames on these. We can't have that, I'm afraid."

She signalled to another helper. "Myrtle, more late arrivals here, love. Can you deal with name tags for them, please?"

Myrtle came over, grumbling. "I wish

they wouldn't keep sending extra kids at the last minute without telling us."

"My real name's Michael Winter," said Worm helpfully as Myrtle began to write out new labels. "And he's Ryan Thomas."

"And what's your proper name, er, Jacko?" she asked.

"Charles . . . Charles Jackson," he said, squirming. The others knew how much he disliked his name. Even most of the teachers called him Jacko.

Myrtle fastened the tags round their necks and they rejoined the queue. "Everything will be all right," she said, trying to comfort them. "It'll be much better for you away from all these nasty bombs."

"Can you tell us where we'll be going?" Jacko asked.

She shook her head. "Sorry, Charlie, I don't know. But I'm sure you'll be very well looked after, wherever it is."

The train carriage was unlike anything the boys had seen before. They shuffled along a narrow corridor, passing several compartments that were already full of children. A guard slid open a door and showed them into another identical compartment with two long bench seats facing each other.

As Jacko and Ryan claimed the places by the window, Worm spotted a newspaper up on the luggage rack next to the football bag. He took it down to look at the date: Sunday, 15th September, 1940.

He showed the others and watched their reactions. Jacko turned pale. Seeing the date in black and white somehow made things seem even worse.

"Right, what are we gonna do now?" muttered Ryan. "Any bright ideas?"

"Well, we can't get off here," said Jacko. "Reckon we wait till the train stops somewhere and then scarper and try to work our way back. What do you say, Worm?"

"I say I'm hungry, Charlie," he replied, pulling out a banana.

Jacko wasn't amused by Worm's cheek. "Where did that come from?"

"Out of my packed lunch. Got good deep pockets, these trousers."

As he peeled away the skin, Worm became aware of many pairs of wide eyes watching his every movement. Then, guiltily, he realized why. He

doubted whether the other children would have seen a banana for months due to food rationing and shortages.

"Er, anybody want a bit?" he offered. By the time the banana returned to him, all that was left was the empty skin.

"Huh! Serves you right," snorted Ryan as a whistle blew, doors slammed shut and the train gave a lurch forwards.

It was a long, slow, uncomfortable journey in the stuffy compartment. Several of the children kept crying, one was sick, and the guards wouldn't let anybody stand in the corridor. There was no chance of escape. Nor did they have any idea where they were or how far they'd travelled. None of the stations they passed had name plates.

"All got taken down so enemy soldiers wouldn't know which route to take if they invaded," Worm explained. "All road signs went too."

"Big help, that," sneered Ryan. "People

must have spent half their time in the war getting lost."

When the train did occasionally halt to offload some of the evacuees, nobody else was allowed to leave their compartment.

"Guess we'll just have to wait till it's our turn," said Jacko, resigned. "God knows where we'll end up now."

Eventually, they found themselves dumped on a draughty platform with about ten other children and then led outside the station. The street scene looked disturbingly familiar to the Rangers, but they were too confused to take it in properly.

A woman in glasses stood in front of them, trying her best to smile a greeting to the nervous newcomers.

"I'm the billeting officer," she announced. "It's my job to find you all a nice new place to live for a while. I know our little village will seem very different to the big city that you're used to, but I hope you will soon feel quite at home here."

Three of the evacuees, at least, were going to feel far more at home than she would ever realize. The woman's smile grew more confident.

"Welcome to Tanfield!"

4 Then and now

The evacuees stood in a line in Tanfield village hall so that people could inspect them and whisper comments about their appearance. Every so often, a choice would be made and one of the children taken away.

"It's like a beauty contest," Worm muttered.

"Bet you're the last to go then," quipped Ryan.

Jacko shook his head. "Incredible to think we were playing footie in here just last weekend, practising for the Sixes."

"Not changed much," Worm observed

sourly. "Don't reckon the walls have had a new coat of paint since the war."

Two more villagers entered the hall. "Sorry we're late," the man said. "Cows take longer to milk now some of our workers have gone off to war."

"Have all the children been spoken for yet?" asked the woman. "Only we'd like to give a home to one or two."

"How about three?" suggested the billeting officer hopefully. "We have three strong boys over there who want to stay together. They might be willing to help out on the farm."

The farmer stroked his chin thoughtfully. "Aye, well, that's a point. We've still got the rest of the harvest to get in, being short-handed."

"That middle one looks just like your cousin George," said his wife, pointing out Jacko. "Isn't that funny?"

"Nay, can't see it myself," he murmured before strolling across to the

Rangers. "How would you fine lads like to live on a farm, eh?"

Ryan and Worm glanced at Jacko, but decided it was wise not to say anything. The farmer carried on speaking.

"Hope you city lads ain't afraid of a spot of hard work."

"I'm not *scared* of hard work," answered Ryan with a cheeky grin. "I just don't like it."

The farmer's wife laughed. "You'll be well fed," she promised. "And our daughter Alice would love having three big brothers to spoil her."

The billeting officer smiled at them. "You're very lucky, boys. Mr and Mrs Probert have a lovely big farm just outside the village. Lots of space to run about and burn up some energy. Off you go now."

The travellers picked up their empty cases and trailed outside.

"This is weird," murmured Jacko as

they clambered up on to the back of the farm truck. "I'm going home."

"How d'yer work that out?" asked Ryan.

"Our place was known as the Probert Farm before Grandad Jackson took it over. These people must be my great grandparents!"

Jacko lapsed into a brooding silence until the truck jolted to a halt in the farmyard. As they jumped down on to the cobbles, a young ginger-haired girl ran out of the house to greet them.

Jacko was rather embarrassed to be introduced to Alice. He didn't know what to say. His usual call of "Hi, Gran!" didn't seem quite appropriate.

Alice volunteered to show the evacuees around the farm as Ryan unpacked the ball and kicked it across the yard. She squealed in delight and dashed after it.

"That feels better," he grinned. "And I've been dying to do something else too. Where's your toilet, my dear Charles?"

Jacko shot him a dirty look. "Upstairs, second on the left," he said and then paused. "Er, wait, I don't know about 1940. Probably one of these buildings in the yard."

"Outside! That's primitive!"

"Don't expect nice soft loo paper either," Worm chuckled. "You might find some torn-up sheets of newspaper there instead, if you're lucky."

"Think I'll hold it for a bit longer," said Ryan, pulling a face.

"Have to be careful what we say while we're here – especially me," said Jacko. "We know far more than we should."

"Yeah, like who won the war, for a kick-off," muttered Ryan.

Jacko was fascinated to see the farm as it used to be. Still carrying the ball, Alice proudly showed them the large barn that had been burnt down ten years before Jacko was born. He smiled to himself. Alice wasn't to know that one day she was going to live on this very spot in Barn Cottage.

And of course there was no pond in the field next to the orchard. Jacko spent some time gazing at the spot where the water should be, lost in thought.

"What's up with you?" grunted Ryan. "It's only a field of spuds, by the look of it."

"Not for much longer it won't be."

"Why, are you gonna set to and dig 'em up right now, Charlie?" he said sarcastically. "We don't have to start work straight away, you know."

Alice interrupted. "It's my birthday tomorrow. I'll be seven!"

"Yeah, I know," said Jacko and then realized his mistake as she stared at him in surprise. "Um . . . I think your mum must have told us."

"Oh! She promised she wouldn't. It was meant to be a secret."

"Not much of a secret," laughed Ryan. "You've just told us too."

"I'm so excited. Mum says I'm going to have a big surprise."

"She's dead right too," murmured Jacko as Alice skipped happily away with the ball. "A very big surprise."

Worm sensed he had something on his mind. "Come on, out with it."

Jacko took a deep breath. "I feared this might happen as soon as we found out the date. Everyone in the family knows about Alice's seventh birthday.

On Monday morning, the sixteenth of September 1940 – eight o'clock, to be precise – a German plane dropped a bomb on our farm and it landed right there. Right on top of Alice. . ."

He pointed into the field and his friends' mouths gaped open.

"It left a crater so big," Jacko went on, "that my great grandparents made it into a pond."

"Thanks for the advance warning," said Ryan. "If they're gonna start bombing this place, we're well out of it. We can leg it after dark."

"Don't be stupid," snapped Worm.

"Who are you calling stupid?"

"You! Don't you see? Little Alice is Jacko's grandma. If she gets killed by this bomb, he's had it too."

"Worm's right," Jacko said quietly. "It'd mean my dad wouldn't exist and so neither would I. . ."

He let that mind-boggling fact sink in

before continuing. "I guess I'd just be wiped from the records somehow. You two wouldn't have heard of me and somebody else would be captain of Tanfield Rangers."

"A fate worse than death," murmured Worm.

"What, not being captain of Rangers?" said Ryan.

"No, never being born in the first place!"

5 Till death do us part

The bedroom was in darkness. The heavy blackout curtain across the window prevented any moonlight from lifting the gloom that had descended upon the three time travellers.

Jacko was the only one lying in a proper bed. The others had to make do with mattresses on the linoleum floor. He had pulled rank on his teammates, not only as captain, but also because this was his own bedroom. He gazed up at the sloping, white-plastered roof above his bed, thinking how strange it looked without all his football posters stuck on it.

"Seems like we've got a date with destiny in the morning," said Worm.

"You two haven't," Jacko corrected him. "But I have. The story goes – the way Gran tells it, anyway – that she was saved by *one* of the evacuees, not all three of them."

"Could be me who rescues her in the nick of time," said Ryan.

"'Fraid not. It's already written in the script. It was the one called Charles. Both me and Dad were named after him."

"That means you're really named after yourself! Spooky!"

"Well, I never realized till today that I was this Charlie in the story, did I? It's not exactly something you expect to crop up when it all happened so long ago."

"Tomorrow," Worm reminded him gently.

"Yeah, right, tomorrow."

"A man's gotta do what a man's gotta do!" drawled Ryan, putting on his best tough-guy, film actor's voice.

"Guess so. You can't go mucking about with history, in spite of what old Worm likes to think."

"I never said you should. But the fact we're here means we're bound to influence things."

"But that's why we *are* here. We're *meant* to be here. We're just playing our roles in the script."

"You'd better not oversleep, then," said Worm. "If you go and miss your cue, you can tear up that script of yours."

Jacko was too terrified even to close his eyes in case he fell asleep. It could be the last thing that he ever did.

He was up and dressed even before the first rays of the rising sun signalled the dawn of a new day. Alice's fateful birthday. His clumping about the room made sure that the other two stirred as well.

"My mouth feels like the bottom of a bird cage," grumbled Ryan.

"You should have packed your toothbrush," said Worm.

"Think I might start carrying one around with me on Rangers tours. You never know where you might end up."

"Let's go and see if my great grandad needs any help," said Jacko, drawing back the curtain. "Cows probably need milking or something."

Ryan yawned. "Just the way I like to start every day. Get up in the middle of the night to go and milk the cows."

"Or clean out the pigsty," added Worm.

"Don't put any ideas into his head."

It was half-past seven when the boys were called in from the milking shed to have their breakfast in the warm kitchen. Alice passed them on the way, carrying the football and a small basket.

"Happy birthday, Alice," Worm greeted her.

She gave them a toothy grin. "I'm going down to the orchard to get some apples for my teacher and my friends at school."

Alice danced off across the yard, bouncing the ball on the cobbles. It was too big for her to control but she loved its patterned markings.

"I think we can say goodbye to that ball," said Worm. "We'll have to give it to her as a birthday present – if the bomb doesn't get it first."

"No way! Dad'll have a fit if we lose this one as well," said Ryan, referring to all the other footballs that had gone missing on their various travels. "Why don't we just simply stop her going into the field? That'd save a lot of trouble all round."

"The script!" hissed Worm. "Charlie's sticking to his gran's story of what happened. No ad-libbing allowed."

Jacko pulled a face. He was already fed up with them calling him Charlie. "What would we say? 'Don't go picking apples because a naughty German pilot is going to drop a bomb on you'? Come off it!"

"Reckon you quite fancy playing the big hero really, don't you, Charlie?" Ryan sneered, twanging Jacko's braces against his chest.

"Ow! That hurt."

"Especially 'cos you know it all ends happily."

"That's just where you're wrong," Jacko replied seriously. "I haven't told you the whole story, yet. I left out one important detail – this Charlie kid gets himself killed. . ."

He walked calmly into the kitchen, leaving his mates rooted to the spot in shock.

"Eat up, you two," urged Mrs Probert. "Your breakfast's going cold."

Ryan and Worm had been exchanging looks with each other and also with Jacko throughout the meal. They'd hardly tasted the bacon and eggs.

"Sorry about the things I said, Jacko. . ." whispered Ryan when Mrs Probert left the room. He tailed off. He didn't really know what to say next.

"It's OK, doesn't matter," Jacko said

with a shrug. "I've just got to go through with it. Been thinking it over all night. There's no way out."

"But it might mean this is going to keep happening for ever," Worm cut in, still wrestling with the problem. "Y'know, like some kind of time loop – like a series of action replays. Alice lives, you get born, you come back to save her, you die, she lives. . ."

"And what are we gonna tell your parents when we get back?" said Ryan, white-faced. "Or even your gran?"

Jacko put down his knife and fork. "Tell them it was worth it."

Mrs Probert returned to the kitchen at that moment and glanced at the clock on the shelf. "Tut! Ten to eight already. Where's that girl got to? She's going to be late for school. Charles, could you pop down to the orchard to hurry her up? Do you remember where it is?"

Jacko nodded. "Don't worry, I know

the way," he said, scraping his chair back across the stone-flagged floor. "I'll go get her for you."

His teammates rose, too, but Mrs Probert was quick to push them back down. "You finish your breakfast. No need for you all to go. Don't run, Charles, or you'll get indigestion."

"That's the least of his worries," murmured Worm.

Jacko forced a smile. "See ya, guys – later on sometime maybe."

"You couldn't have timed it better coming here," Mrs Probert said when he'd gone. "You'll be able to join in the fun of Alice's birthday party this afternoon. She doesn't know yet that we've bought her a pony."

As she went to busy herself at the sink, Worm stood up.

"Where yer going?" hissed Ryan. "You know what Jacko said."

"That's why I'm going. We can't just

sit here while he dices with death. We've got to do something."

"What?"

"I don't know – just something."

"What's the matter, Michael?" asked Mrs Probert as he reached the door.

"Er, thought I heard a plane. Just wanted to check what it was."

"There's no need to worry, love. We're in no danger here. . ."

Worm had already disappeared – and Ryan bolted after him.

"Boys!" she exclaimed. "I'm so glad we had a little girl."

Jacko was racing along a rutted track, taking a short cut he knew would bring him out near the orchard. The blood was pounding in his ears, but he could hear a droning noise in the sky, a noise that was getting nearer and nearer. And there she was.

Alice was leaving the orchard with a basketful of apples and picking her way around the edge of the potato crop. The droning was now even louder and he saw her shield her eyes from the sun to look up.

"It's a German bomber!" he yelled. "Get down!"

She laughed. "Don't be silly. We don't have Germans on our farm."

Jacko was gasping for breath as he stumbled across the field furrows. Alice could see the panic in his eyes as he approached and she screamed. Jacko reached her at full speed, almost

knocking her over, but he managed to grab her with both arms. He lifted her up off her feet and kept on running, sending the apples and the football flying into the air.

"Oh God, I've left it too late," he cried, finding Alice heavier than he expected. "I'm not gonna make it in time. . ."

6 Many happy returns?

Worm and Ryan found the farmer in one of the cowsheds and gabbled out about the plane.

"Aye, be one of ours, don't you fret," he said, unconcerned.

"It's not! It's not!" Worm screamed, dragging him away from his work. "It's the enemy! C'mon, Alice is out in the open."

Mr Probert rushed outside into the yard. The plane was now right overhead and they all began to run towards the orchard.

There was a bone-chilling, whistling sound through the air.

"Bomb!" shrieked Ryan.

They threw themselves to the ground which shook and rumbled underneath them like an earthquake as the bomb landed. The blast made their ears throb, but they were up on their feet again and running even before the tremors died away. The plane disappeared into the distance.

"Alice! Alice!" her father shouted. "Where are you?"

Silence. Apart from the terrible cacophony of cackling, snorting and bellowing noises of all the farm animals.

The three of them finally pulled up beside what was once the potato crop, appalled by the devastation. Steam and smoke swirled out of a huge crater, and many trees in the neighbouring orchard had been uprooted. It was also raining dirt and potatoes. One thumped down on to Worm's shoulder but he barely noticed.

They desperately scanned the field for any sign of movement, but there was nothing to be seen. Nobody could have survived such an explosion at close quarters.

"Jacko!" Worm called out. "Jacko! Alice! Are you all right?"

Still no reply. "Perhaps they're somewhere in the orchard," panted Ryan, grasping at a thin strand of hope.

"Wait, what's that?" said Worm.

A faint, muffled cry was coming from the far edge of the field. They set off at a gallop and reached a ditch by the collapsed wall of the orchard. Together, they scrabbled frantically at the mounds of earth, leaves, branches and stonework piled on top of it.

Mr Probert was soon cradling his whimpering daughter in his arms. "I've lost all my apples!" she wailed. "And Charlie's deaded."

It looked as if Alice was right. Buried beneath more of the debris was Jacko's spread-eagled body, face down in the ditch. As his friends cleared away the last branches that covered him, Ryan let out a whoop of relief.

"He moved. He's alive!"

Jacko stirred again and moaned as they tried to turn him over. "Ugh! Gerroff, will yer," he slurred.

"He's alive, OK," grunted Worm.

"Welcome back from the dead, Jacko."

The farmer gave Jacko a rough examination. "No bones broken. You're a lucky lad. And a brave one, too. Can't thank you enough, Charlie."

"My ankle feels like it's on fire."

"Bet you've twisted it," said Ryan as Mr Probert went to comfort Alice once more. "Bang goes your footie. That's you out of the Sixes now."

"Better than being killed, though, eh?" said Worm. "How's the scriptwriter going to deal with Charlie surviving?"

Jacko looked suddenly sheepish. "Soz, I was lying about that bit."

"What! You mean you knew you weren't going to die?"

"You are now," hissed Ryan. "'Cos I'm gonna kill you myself for playing a dirty trick like that on us."

"I just couldn't resist it. Guess I was trying to get you both back for all those

Charlie taunts. But you should have seen your faces!"

"It's not funny," growled Worm, surprising Jacko with his fierceness. "Don't ever take liberties with time travel like that again. You're tempting fate. It's just asking for trouble."

"I got it," he admitted, still shaken up. "I really thought I was a gonner back there."

Mr Probert carried the injured Jacko back towards the farmhouse while Worm gave Alice a piggyback until her

mother came running up to take over. Ryan was trailing behind and picked up a charred remnant from the rim of the smouldering bomb crater. It was a small piece of leather.

"Dad's not gonna be too pleased about this," he murmured, throwing the scrap of football away.

"Right, all set, lads?" said Mr Probert. "Got your gas masks and stuff?"

Ryan patted his empty case. "Yeah, didn't take us long to pack."

It had taken the evacuees three days, however, to persuade the Proberts to let them return to the capital. They had insisted it was the best possible way of rewarding them for saving Alice's life.

Jacko had been resting his bandaged ankle for most of this time while his pals were hard at work in the fields. The farmer was now taking some of the harvest to market in a nearby town and had agreed to put the boys on the London train. He didn't want to risk meeting the billeting officer at Tanfield station.

Mrs Probert dabbed at her eyes. "We still wish you'd change your minds and stay with us on the farm. It'd be much safer here. . ."

She paused. "Aye, well, you know what we mean," added her husband. "We'll be thinking about you every time we hear of another raid on London."

"We'll be fine, don't worry," said Jacko, trying to reassure his great grandparents. "We know what we're doing. I can't really explain, but we'll soon be well out of reach of any German bombers."

Alice was hugging her mother's apron and snuffling. "You'll come back and see us, won't you?" she begged.

"Yes, I promise," Jacko replied, taking a last look round at his future home.

"I'll be back one day. You haven't seen the last of me."

She trotted forward to whisper in his ear before he was helped up on to the truck to sit among the vegetables.

"You've got those things I gave you yesterday, haven't you?"

He nodded, picturing each of the objects lying hidden in the darkness, as if frozen in time. "All stashed away in a safe place, thanks."

She seemed pleased. "Do you know what I've decided to call my pony?"

"Adolf?" he suggested to tease her.

Alice giggled, blushed, and then shared her secret before running off.

"What was that all about?" asked Worm as they were jostled about on the slithering cargo along the rutted farm track.

"Oh, just about names. By the way, did I ever tell you two that I was christened Charles Michael Ryan?" he said, grinning at the astonished looks on their faces. "So now you can see why I prefer Jacko!"

"These carrots are lumpy," muttered Ryan to cover his embarrassment.

Hours later, after a tiring journey of many delays, the travellers trudged along the platform at St Pancras station. They were just about to hand in the tickets that Mr Probert had bought for them when suddenly an awful wailing sound started up. People broke into a run.

"What the hell is that racket?" demanded Ryan.

"Air-raid siren," said Worm. "This is the Blitz, remember."

They were swept up in the crowd making for the shelter of the Tube station, Jacko still limping as he tried to hurry.

"Well, this is where the time-slip happened," he said as they reached the escalator. "D'yer think it'll reverse itself?"

Worm shrugged. "It's worked like that before on our other trips, coming back to the same spot."

"OK, then, let's go," cried Ryan. "Back to the future."

They stepped on to the moving wooden staircase and began their descent, expecting any moment that their surroundings would flicker and change. The lower they got, the more anxious they became.

"Nothing's happening!" exclaimed Jacko.

It was their worst nightmare. They gathered at the bottom, wondering what to do next, as everyone else scurried by.

"Let's try again," said Worm, struggling to stay calm. "Maybe we weren't quite synchronized or something."

They made for the "up" escalator, but found their path barred by a policeman. "Sorry, lads. No exit. There's another Jerry raid on."

"But we've got to go up," pleaded Ryan. "We shouldn't be here."

Worm pulled his teammates away. "It's no use arguing. I reckon the only way is back up the 'down' escalator. C'mon, follow me."

The boys launched up the steps, cursed by the people coming down as their suitcases bashed into knees. But it was simply too crowded. They were only about a third of the way up when their progress was halted and they allowed themselves to be carried back downwards.

Worm saw the policeman waiting for them.

"That copper's there," he cried out. "Keep going. Get up, get up."

In desperation, they attempted to burrow a path through the bodies, but they made little headway. For every step they climbed, the escalator conveyed them further down. It was a losing battle. Their legs weakened and they began to feel dizzy. Their vision clouded over. . .

As their senses returned, the escalator dumped them unceremoniously back on to the bottom corridor. It was almost empty. Only Dazza was there, gawping at them, speechless. Then the photographer strode up.

"So that's where you are," he fumed. "You had no right going off in those clothes. Where've you been?"

"Er . . . good question," said Worm hesitantly. "Unfortunately, I haven't got a good answer right now. You'd never believe it, anyway."

The photographer wasn't amused. And nor was the next person who arrived on the scene. "Found you, have we?" said Mr Thomas. "And where's the ball, may I ask, Ryan?"

"Um . . . well," his son murmured, stalling for time while he considered how best to explain its loss. "It kind of got burst. . ."

"Burst! You've only been out of sight for a few minutes."

"Somebody else got hold of it, you see, Dad – and then all of a sudden there was this great big bang. . ."

7 Group games

More bad news was to follow for the team managers of Tanfield Rangers. Not only had they lost a football, they'd lost their captain too.

Jacko was given a fitness test when they arrived at the sports centre after lunch. He tried to mask the pain of his ankle injury but it was clear that he wasn't in any state to play in the Sixes tournament.

"We'll just have to manage without you," sighed Mr Stoppard, the co-manager and father of the team's vice-captain, Stopper. "You'd only make the damage worse and end up being out of action for even longer."

Mr Thomas was less sympathetic. "What a stupid thing to go and do, messing about on the escalator and knackering your ankle."

Ryan cut in. "We're not a one-man team, Dad. We can still win the Sixes, even without Charlie . . . er, I mean, Jacko."

The rest of the squad already knew the real reason for Jacko's injury. Over lunch, the three travellers had told the others of their wartime experiences. Their teammates had no difficulty in believing the story. They were all veterans of past and future time-adventures.

"I bet that was the only bomb in the whole war to drop on Tanfield," chuckled Stopper. "And trust you lot to be there at the time."

"Jacko not only saved his gran's life,"

Worm pointed out, "he saved his own too. Worth the sacrifice of missing the footie, eh?"

"Worm made a sacrifice as well," added Jacko, playfully waggling a banana from his packed lunch under the defender's nose. "He gave away his own banana to the starving evacuees on the train!"

"Just doing my bit for the war effort," Worm said, affecting modesty.

The managers gathered the players together after the warm-up session.

"The draw's been made for the groups," Mr Thomas informed them. "It's not come out too bad for us. We've got the Likely Lads first, then the Tigers, which saves the toughest game till last – against United."

"We'll start off by playing a basic 2-2-1 formation," said Mr Stoppard. "Rakesh and Anil, you'll be in midfield, but make sure you support Ryan in attack whenever you can."

"Just give me the ball and I'll do the rest," boasted Ryan.

It was said with a grin, but they all knew he meant business. Their top striker never passed the ball when he sniffed a goal-scoring chance.

Stopper, now wearing the captain's armband, was the team's main defender, but he wasn't expecting to be too busy in the opening match. Rangers had played against the Likely Lads in the Saturday tournament and they were confident of victory.

That confidence was soon shaken. After both Ryan and Anil had gone close to putting Rangers ahead – Anil hitting a post – they fell behind instead to a soft goal. Worm was caught in possession on the right-hand side and the ball was swept across to an unmarked attacker. Dazza was out of position and had no chance of stopping the shot.

The Lads defended their surprise lead

with a mixture of good teamwork and good fortune. It took Rangers most of the second half to put matters right. Substitute Speedie replaced Anil to partner Ryan up front and it was from his burst forward that the equalizer at last came.

His pace and dribbling skills created space for Ryan to shoot, but the ball cannoned off a defender. Speedie finished off what he'd started, lashing the rebound past the keeper into the net with great glee.

That was the end of the scoring. A single point was a poor return for all their efforts, but they heard that United and Tigers had drawn 1–1 too.

During the rest period, the Rangers watched a game in the other group. The College, their friends and rivals from previous encounters, looked in fine form and chalked up a 3–0 win. Whizzer, the captain, scored twice.

"Let's hope we don't have to deal with

him again today," said Rakesh. "He always gives us the run-around."

Rangers soon had other worries on their mind – how to tame the Tigers. And their cause wasn't helped by Rakesh's error of judgement in the very first minute of the match. Perhaps he was still thinking about Whizzer.

Dazza had parried an awkward, skimming shot, but the ball spun loose towards a Tigers attacker lurking on the edge of the semi-circular goal area. Rakesh panicked and intercepted the ball before it came out.

The referee instantly blew his whistle. "Penalty!" he announced. "Defender went into the area to play the ball."

Rakesh held his head in his hands, trying not to hear the names that Dazza was calling him. As the ball was placed on the penalty spot, Dazza composed himself. He'd sort Rakesh out later if this cost them a goal.

It didn't. Dazza guessed correctly, diving to his left to palm the penalty away to safety. As the cheers rang out, Anil steered the ball along the boards at the side of the pitch up to Ryan, catching the Tigers off guard. Ryan sprinted clear, but his shooting let him down for once. He shot wildly over the low crossbar and then kicked down one of the boards in frustration. His tantrum earned him a ticking-off from the referee.

The misses set the tone for the rest of the game. Chance after chance went begging at both ends, with Rangers grateful for an inspired display by Dazza. He made a series of outstanding saves to keep a clean sheet, but his teammates couldn't find the net either.

"What was the score?" asked Jacko, hobbling back from a spying mission.

"Nil-nil," said Worm. "Dazza played a blinder. What about United?"

"Stuffed the Lads 3–1," he reported,

but tried to sound optimistic. "They're good, but not unbeatable. I reckon their keeper's a bit dodgy. He was at fault for the goal that he let in."

United's victory put them two points clear of Rangers and Tigers at the top of the group table. With only two teams due to qualify for the knockout stage of the competition, Rangers were placed second purely on alphabetical order.

Group A

	P.	W.	D.	L.	F.	A.	Pts.
United	2	1	1	0	4	2	4
Rangers	2	0	2	0	1	1	2
Tigers	2	0	2	0	1	1	2
Likely Lads	2	0	1	1	2	4	1

8 In and out

"This is the crunch game," stressed Stopper as they prepared to face United. "We must win it to make sure we go through. A draw's no good."

"Dead right," agreed Ryan. "The best form of defence is attack."

Ryan was addicted to scoring goals and he hadn't yet enjoyed the buzz that hitting the net gave him. He wanted to test the United keeper out as soon as possible. Receiving a pass from Worm, he let fly from an acute angle, but the boy was alert to the danger and had the shot well covered.

For most of the first half, however, Dazza was the busier of the two goalkeepers. United's slick-passing moves forced Speedie and Rakesh to spend more time helping out in defence than feeding Ryan's addiction. Worm and Stopper were kept at full stretch, and Rangers had to rely on Dazza's agility to rescue them when the United attackers did escape their markers.

Even Dazza had the woodwork to thank for sparing his blushes once. He allowed the ball to slip from his grasp and watched agonizingly as it rolled towards the net. His prayers were answered. The ball clunked against the foot of the post and stayed there. Nobody could enter the area to tap it in and Dazza strolled over and picked it up.

"No sweat," he said, acting cool.

But it wasn't all one-way traffic. Just before the interval, the white-shirted

Rangers broke through United's multi-coloured ranks and almost snatched the lead. Speedie's shot looked a certain goal until the keeper dived to his right to tip the ball over the bar.

"Huh! Some dodgy keeper!" Ryan snorted at half-time.

Jacko shrugged. He just wished he could be on the pitch, driving his team forward, instead of being a helpless spectator. And even a hopeless spy.

"We've got to take a few risks now," decided Mr Thomas. "All-out attack, lads. Go for goals!"

The gamble to take Worm off nearly proved an instant disaster. Dazza had very little defensive cover left and only Stopper's last-ditch lunge to block a goalbound shot kept Rangers on level terms.

Then Ryan struck at last. He intercepted a wayward, underarm throw from the United goalkeeper and made him pay the price for his carelessness. Ryan swept on to the ball, controlled it with one deft touch and stroked it into the net with another to break the deadlock.

He celebrated in his usual flamboyant style, punching the air, and jumped right over the boards to give both Worm and Jacko a big hug.

"That one's for Alice!" he cried.

His dad looked puzzled. "Who's this Alice? His girlfriend at school?"

Worm grinned. "No, Jacko's grandma!"

Mr Thomas was even more puzzled. "Crazy kids!" he muttered.

"Concentrate!" yelled Mr Stoppard. "Don't relax. Let's have another."

Rangers duly obliged. United seemed to go to pieces after conceding such a sloppy goal. They started arguing among themselves, blaming each other for mistakes, and Rangers took full advantage of their disarray.

Rakesh, Anil and Speedie linked up in Rangers' best move of the game, leaving Ryan with the goal at his mercy. The goal-addict was in no mood to kick the habit. He booted the ball instead with tremendous power and it pierced the gap between the groping keeper and his near post.

United had no response to Ryan's second strike and Rangers' 2–0 victory saw them leapfrog their opponents to grab top spot in the group.

"Lucky for United that Tigers could only draw again," Stopper remarked, studying the tables in the results area. "Semi-finals, here we come."

"Yeah, *and* we've avoided Whizzer," said a relieved Rakesh. "Group winners play the other runners-up."

Stopper grinned. "Suits me. We'll save College for the Final."

Group A

	P.	W.	D.	L.	F.	A.	Pts.
Rangers	3	1	2	0	3	1	5
United	3	1	1	1	4	4	4
Tigers	3	0	3	0	2	2	3
Likely Lads	3	0	2	1	3	5	2

Group B

	P.	W.	D.	L.	F.	A.	Pts.
College	3	2	1	0	6	2	7
Aces	3	2	0	1	4	2	6
Dynamos	3	0	2	1	2	3	2
Double Six	3	0	1	2	1	6	1

The Rangers players felt drained after the United game. It had taken more out of them than they realized, and the semi-final clash with Anglesey Aces seemed almost like an anti-climax.

"You've done well to qualify, unbeaten, without Jacko," Mr Stoppard said. "But this is no time to let up. The hard work starts now."

"What I really want is a nice long rest," groaned Ryan, more tired than most after his days spent toiling in the fields.

The match did not start well. Ryan whirled round after scoring, arm raised in delight, only to discover that the referee had awarded a free-kick to the Aces. The pass from Speedie had gone over head height.

To add to Rangers' disappointment, the Aces used the free-kick to launch a successful attack of their own. The kick was taken quickly and threaded through to the unmarked winger whose shot clipped Stopper on the knee. The deflection was a cruel blow, sending the ball skidding past the wrong-footed Dazza.

The Rangers pressed hard for the equalizer, pinning their opponents on the defensive, until the Aces caught them on the break again. They gave Dazza his least favourite job to do for a second time – picking the ball out of the back of his net.

This was where Rangers missed Jacko's strength and inspiration. He was at his best when the going got tough, and they were certainly facing an uphill battle now. There seemed to be no way past the huge Aces' goalie. He kept swallowing up their shots like a black hole.

It was late in the game when Rangers at last managed to strike back. Ryan bustled past two challenges to make space for a shot which bounced back off the boards and Anil somehow squeezed the ball underneath the goalie's diving bulk.

The goal gave Rangers fresh hope, even though the minutes were steadily ticking away. They were well used to time being against them. The Aces were desperate now to hear the final whistle, but they still had to suffer another heart-stopping moment. Speedie's low drive hit

the keeper's legs and looped up on to the top of the crossbar before going out of play.

Seconds later, it was all over – Rangers had lost 2–1. It took quite a while for the sad fact to sink in that they were out of the tournament.

"Bet we'd have won if Jacko had been fit," moaned Anil.

Worm nodded. "Can't be helped. It was an old war wound. He was lucky to live to tell the tale."

Rangers stayed to watch the Final and cheer on their College pals who had defeated United 3–1 in the other semi. College repeated that scoreline against the weary Aces, winning the match comfortably in the end. Whizzer himself scored two of the goals and then held aloft the Sunday trophy in triumph.

"Pity that wasn't us," said Jacko, "but I'm pleased for Whizzer. He deserved it.

He's got to be the star player of the festival this weekend."

"Right, let's hit the road, guys," said Mr Thomas. "Time to go home."

Ryan grinned at Worm. "Little does he know that we already nipped back there earlier!"

"We won't be arriving at Tanfield station this time, though. It got knocked down years ago after it closed."

"No wonder we didn't recognize the place."

"At least we've got proof that we *were* really there," added Worm.

"Yeah, my sore ankle," Jacko chipped in.

"And also the buried treasure."

"If it's still there," said Ryan. "If a whole station can disappear, so can that."

"We'll soon find out," Jacko reminded them. "Don't forget our date with Alice on Wednesday. It's Gran's sixty-fifth birthday!"

Postscript:
Buried Treasure

At five o'clock on Wednesday afternoon, the three Time Rangers pushed open the door of a ramshackle brick building near the pond on Jackson's Farm. Light streamed inside through the gaps in the roof.

"You sure you haven't been in here to check yet?" demanded Ryan.

"Does it look like it?" said Jacko.

The boys stared in dismay at the piles of junk that had been dumped in the old storehouse and forgotten. It was full of wooden crates, glass jars and rusted machinery. It took them twenty minutes to clear the far corner enough to reveal a small cross scratched on one of the floorboards.

Worm grinned. "X marks the spot – just like in pirate stories!"

Ryan prised up a couple of rotting boards with his bare hands so that the kneeling Jacko could shine his torch into the low floor space.

"Can't see anything," he grunted, squinting down the beam of light. "No, wait – there it is!"

Jacko reached into the hole and pulled out a thin metal tin. He brushed the dirt off it with his sleeve, breathing heavily in excitement.

"Just think – this old tobacco tin has been under there all those years and nobody knew anything about it."

"Well, open it, then," Worm urged. "Don't keep us in suspense."

They were all anxious to find out how well the tin's treasures had survived the passage of time. They were personal souvenirs from Alice, given to them on the evening before they left the Probert Farm.

"Some things to remember me by," she'd said shyly, blushing.

The evacuees had placed the items inside the tin and secretly stowed it away like a time capsule – for hopeful rediscovery by their future selves.

This was the moment of truth. Jacko snapped open the hinged lid of the tin and gazed with a certain awe at the three wartime relics. They were remarkably well preserved.

Jacko lifted out a blackened silver cross and chain. "This was one of Alice's own birthday presents," he murmured. "Gran's told me she had to pretend it was lost in the blast so that she wouldn't get into trouble."

Ryan held up a square piece of cloth, upon which Alice had tried to embroider a football. She had even sewn all their initials around it.

"Made quite a good job of it really, didn't she?" he said. "I mean, considering she was only just seven at the time."

Worm carefully unfolded a faded newspaper cutting from the *Tanfield Gazette* the day after the bombing. They chuckled at the bold headline.

BRAVE EVACUEES SAVE
BIRTHDAY GIRL

Underneath was a photograph of a beaming Alice with her new pony and her three rescuers. The boys read again the article about Charlie's desperate dash across the field as the bomber approached, and how his friends and the farmer had dug him and Alice out of the ditch.

"I've been checking through some old newspapers in the library since we got back," said Worm. "They reckoned the plane was jettisoning its bomb load before trying to limp back to Germany. Never made it home, though. It'd been hit during the night raid and was finished off by a couple of Spitfires as it crossed the coast."

"Yeah, I already know all that. It's family history," smiled Jacko. "C'mon, let's put everything back in the tin. I can't wait to see Gran's face when she opens it herself."

"Won't she recognize ours in the picture?" asked Ryan, worried.

"Nah, the only one that really stands out is the pony's."

Jacko's widowed grandmother was sewing in the kitchen of Barn Cottage as the boys knocked and entered. Alice's mass of ginger hair was now a steely grey.

"Hi, Gran! Happy birthday!" Jacko greeted her, producing the tin from behind his back. "Um, we've found this in one of the outbuildings. Thought it might bring back a few special memories, like, for you. . ."

"I don't recognize it, boys," she said, examining the decorative lid. Alice eased it up gently and then stared in amazement at the tin's contents. Tears began to trickle down her cheeks.

"Oh, my goodness me," she whispered. "Thank you so much, boys.

You have no idea how much these things mean to me."

One by one, she held the precious items in her wrinkled hands.

"This is Jacko," she said suddenly, showing them the photograph.

"Eh?" exclaimed Ryan in alarm.

"My lovely little pony. I named him Jacko after the lad who saved my life. He was called Jackson, too, you know, just like my future husband."

"Life's full of strange coincidences, isn't it, Mrs Jackson?" said Worm innocently.

Alice fell silent for a while, hardly able to believe that she had been reunited with such treasures. Then she peered through her glasses more closely at the boys in the picture.

"Do you know, another strange thing is that these evacuees are the spit of you three lads?" she mused. "Now isn't that incredible?"

She was talking to herself. The boys had already gone, slipping away to leave Alice in her own private little wonderland.

Alice sighed and shook her head. "Curiouser and curiouser. . ."

Alternative and Activist Media

Mitzi Waltz

Edinburgh University Press

For the Independent Media Centre movement worldwide.

Edinburgh University Press Ltd
22 George Square, Edinburgh

Typeset in Janson and Neue Helvetica
by Norman Tilley Graphics, and
printed and bound in Great Britain
by MPG Books Ltd, Bodmin, Cornwall

A CIP record for this book is available from the British Library

ISBN 0 7486 1957 7 (hardback)
ISBN 0 7486 1958 5 (paperback)

Contents

Illustrations

Acknowledgements

So many people have helped in the production of this book that it's hard to know where to start saying thank you.

I'll begin with my parents, since they were there at the beginning: Sam and Mary Ann Smith, who always encouraged me to read and write, and through whose mailbox I received my first manila envelopes of underground newspapers and punk fanzines.

Then there are those who encouraged me to get involved in the alternative and activist press: Brad Trevathan and other high-school friends who participated in *The Tilghman Hell* adventure; Jaime Trujillo, whose *Mutual Oblivion* fanzine was the first to publish my work; the late Tim Yohannon, my friend, mentor, and companion on late-night trips to see the buffalo in Golden Gate Park as well as shows at Gilman Street; and Aaron Cometbus, for being instrumental in changing my life through the zine world without even knowing it.

Next are the teachers and editors who have guided me as a professional: Juan Gonzales of *El Tecolote*, who encouraged me at City College of San Francisco; Michael Moore at *Mother Jones*; Betty Medsger and John Burks at San Francisco State University; Sarah Colm at *The Tenderloin Times*; Henry Norr at *MacWEEK*; and Jim Redden at *PDXS*, among others.

Of course, I couldn't have found the time to finish this if not for the patience of my partner in all things, Steve Schultz, and my children, Ian and Carmen.

And finally, there are all the people who contributed their time, words, and critiques to this project: my editor, Valerie Alia; Sarah Edwards at Edinburgh University Press; and everyone who took the time to talk to me – Najma Abdullah, Chris Atton, Ed Baxter, Bliz, Daniel Clark, Michael Dean, Steve Dunifer, Friba, Martin James, Michael Lahey, Lynne Lowe, Justin Marler, Nic Millington, Paul O'Connor, Barbara O'Leary, Jerod Poore, Jim Redden, Marleen Stikker, Rena Tangens, Laura Tisoncik, Vicki Travis, V. Vale, Ken Waschberger, Richard Waters, and many more. I hope I haven't forgotten anyone.

To all of you: thank you.

Preface

The spectacle is not a collection of images; it is a social relation between people that is mediated by images. The spectacle cannot be understood as a mere visual deception produced by mass-media technologies. It is a worldview that has actually been materialized, a view of a world that has become objective.

Guy Debord, *The Society of the Spectacle*, 1967

This book arrives at a moment when Debord's 'society of the spectacle' seems to be an inescapable construct.

Communication has become a precious, and precarious, commodity. As Robert McChesney writes, 'journalism which, in theory, should inspire political involvement tends to strip politics of meaning and promote a broad depoliticization'.[1] Writing, speaking, or acting critically can once again result in arrest, even in the 'democratic' West, without public outcry.

The act of speaking truth to power currently means confronting the full force of the marketised mass media, the corporate public relations process, and crushing apathy among those for whom the spectacle of modern life has been confused with its reality from their earliest moments spent gazing into the depths of the glowing box that dominates family life.

In these conditions, no one should be surprised that most media studies texts concentrate on the mass media: the popular information and entertainment products of corporations through which our mediated culture itself is produced, consumed and recycled. These media products are ubiquitous, and as the concentration of media ownership increases, even fewer voices can be heard within this hegemonic mainstream.

However, either despite this situation or because of it, alternative and activist media remain, opening up cracks in the mass-media monolith through which strange flowers grow. The mass-media monopoly has also brought with it an increase in media literacy, giving audiences more tools for semiotic and active engagement with media. This book describes and analyses media that these engaged audiences can find elsewhere, and discusses some of the counter-hegemonic strategies and practices of engaged media producers. It brings diverse voices and concepts from outside the commercial media world to the fore, challenging the mass-media spectacle on all fronts.

This book is designed to serve university media studies, print and broadcast journalism, cultural studies, and media sociology courses, but I hope it will also be of interest to readers who are not involved in formal academic study. You don't need a journalism degree to write what you see happening around you, and with modern technology you can apply yourself to radio, television, and online media as well.

Chapter 1 defines 'alternative and activist media', and considers the need for non-mainstream publications. It introduces the populations who seek out or create alternative media: socially marginalised or dissenting groups, subcultures and others who inhabit liminal spaces, and people who want access to information not available through the mass media. It will also examine the 'information for action' orientation of much alternative media, which places it in opposition to the mass media's 'information for consumption'.

Chapter 2 puts the emergence and persistence of alternative and activist media in context, calling into question media analysis that looks strictly at mass media, and posing the possibility and reality of counter-hegemonic actions and actors. It includes an overview of key theorists as regards alternative media and media activism. Chapter 3 looks specifically at media participation and consumption by marginalised audiences.

The following five chapters look at alternative and activist media formats and rationales in the realms of radio, video, film, print, and digital media, concentrating on real-world practices and projects.

In Chapter 9, the border between alternative and activist media and the mass media is probed, revealing areas of contention, reflection, and recuperation. Chapter 10 concludes this exploration with a look at the future, based on an examination of current trends and technologies.

At all points readers are encouraged to do more than analyse and understand these media forms – they are urged to engage with the idea of making their *own* media, and offered tools, ideas, and inspiration to do so. I would like to challenge you to make the media you want to see, communicate the realities of your life as you're living it, and reach out to others by doing so, rather than playing the part of passive consumers, or even of 'active participants' in mediated interactions scripted by others. Moving from theory to practice is personally satisfying, socially responsible, and the only way to flip the mass-media machine's 'off' switch.

Mitzi Waltz

1 Who needs an alternative? An introduction to the role of alternative and activist media

A few media conglomerates now exercise a near-monopoly over television news. There is always a risk that news organizations can emphasize or ignore stories to serve their corporate purpose. But the risk is far greater when there are no independent competitors to air the side of the story the corporation wants to ignore.

Ted Turner, founder of CNN and chairman of Turner Enterprises[1]

Thousands of hardy, grassroots people have been working steadily and creatively over the years in every area of media, and the result of their combined efforts is that a new media force is now flowering coast to coast – a force of hundreds of media outlets that is unabashedly progressive, fiercely independent, diverse, dispersed, and democratic. Some of these outlets are nationally known, others only locally known; some are brand new, others have been plugging away for decades. But the significant thing is that, collectively, they are a force to be reckoned with, celebrated, strategically deployed and deliberately expanded.

Jim Hightower, author of *Thieves in High Places* and other books[2]

Two visions of the state of today's media … which is correct?

The answer is: both. By any measure, it's true that the mainstream media has never been concentrated in fewer hands, has never been more in thrall to corporate power, and has never been less trusted by its readers and viewers. But it's also true that the media outside the mainstream has expanded to a huge extent in the past few decades. Indeed, according to an annual report on the state of the news media in America, alternative, ethnic, and online media are the only news outlets gaining in audience numbers.[3]

Some, like Jim Hightower, argue that these alternative and activist sources of information actually reach more people than their corporate counterparts. Others are less sure about their impact.

1

What is alternative media?

One area of controversy is how the term 'alternative media' is defined. This has long been an area of contention for media theorists. Richard Abel has forthrightly stated that it is undefinable.[4] Chris Atton presents several different sets of criteria, all of which differ in at least some aspects. In his critique of these definitions, he notes that some are predicated on incorrect assumptions – for example, the Royal Commission on the Press has stated that alternative publications deal with 'the opinions of small minorities', while, as Atton points out, gay and lesbian publications are aimed at quite a large minority.[5] Indeed, ethnic minority publications may target a *majority* of readers in some urban areas, in response to these communities being historically underserved by mainstream newspapers and broadcast outlets.

One could choose simply to deconstruct the term 'alternative media' to reveal a basic definition. It describes media that are alternative to, or in opposition to, something else: mass-media products that are widely available and widely consumed. Even a mass-media product like CNN could constitute an 'alternative' in a repressive society where all outside media are banned, such as North Korea. But in situations where a variety of mass-media products is available, those media that provide a different point of view from that usually expressed, that cater to communities not well served by the mass media, or that expressly advocate social change would meet this very basic definition.

So what does alternative media look like in the latter, more typical situation? Perhaps the first image that comes to mind is some sort of explicitly counterculture 'underground' newspaper run by a hippie collective in the 1960s. Maybe you're familiar with union newsletters, low-budget literary magazines, digital radio stations that serve audiences dedicated to marginal musical styles, or newspapers put out by radical political parties. Or maybe what you think of is a web site run by and for environmental activists, a home-made punk fanzine, or a feminist radio show broadcast on a community-owned station. They are all alternative in the simple sense of covering topics that are not an everyday focus for typical newspapers, magazines, or broadcast media. However, only some of these media products would fit an even more stringent definition of alternative media, as only some of them are created and disseminated in ways that are radically different from mainstream business practices.

Michael Albert argues that to be 'alternative', alternative media can't just be a product that differs from the norm in content, or that caters to a somewhat non-mainstream audience with otherwise typical content.

'Being alternative as an institution must have to do with how the institution is organized and works,' he says in an article for the activist US publication *Z Magazine*, which he founded. Albert goes on to set out a platform for how a truly alternative media organisation should operate.[6] In Exercise 1.1 at the end of this chapter, you'll be encouraged to explore your own thoughts about his suggestions.

Of course, not everyone agrees with Albert's purist vision. For example, the Comedia group, which undertook an in-depth study of the left alternative press in the UK, has written that alternative and activist media have historically been marginalised by their reluctance to use a capitalist business model or target mass audiences. Comedia argued that if an alternative publication has increased activism as its goal, it should adopt business practices that enable it to reach the widest possible audience.[7] And even Albert suggests that there must be room under the alternative media umbrella for media forms with a unique artistic vision, or those that cater to underserved audiences despite having a corporate business model.

Clemencia Rodríguez has recently put forward a third major definition that tries to find a route around the term 'alternative media' altogether, suggesting that certain types of media be defined solely by their intents, effects, and processes rather than their relationship to mainstream mass media. She argues that the term 'citizens' media' is a better fit, encompassing a means of production characterised by open access and volunteerism, goals involving social change, and a not-for-profit orientation.[8] Such media products would be both alternative and activist, by any definition.

Exercise 1.2 asks you to decide whether specific media organisations and their products meet your own definition of 'alternative', based on your understanding of the differing visions presented in this chapter.

What is activist media?

It's important to understand that 'alternative' and 'activist' do not necessarily mean the same thing. Activist media, as the term implies, encourage readers to get actively involved in social change. They may espouse any political philosophy, from far left to far right – indeed, a broad definition of 'activist' would include media that advocate absolutely mainstream actions, such as voting for the politician of your choice or volunteering for charity.

Some theorists argue that publications promoting such widely accepted forms of social and political activity are not outside the mainstream, and so should not be considered as separate from mass-media products. Tim O'Sullivan, for example, claims that to be 'alternative', a media source must advocate radical social change. He goes on to suggest that such products must also use a 'democratic/collectivist process of production' and pursue new directions for the content they run and/or their design and delivery mechanisms.[9]

Rodríguez's proposed definition of 'citizen's media' expressly rejects products that are not associated with 'progressive' movements or that do not respect diversity. This narrower category would not include racist and far-right media, for example.[10]

Some activist media strive for mainstream appeal, and try to reach a very broad audience. Union magazines, online activist web sites like MoveOn.org or SierraClub.org, and critical documentaries like Michael Moore's *Fahrenheit 911* may take an oppositional stance, and certainly are aimed at social change, but they use mainstream formats, distribution networks, and business models to achieve their goals. Their intention is to make activism mainstream, and their creators ultimately hope that their views will be picked up by the mass media.

Many, but not all, activist media are also alternative media. When activist media advocate left-wing or anarchist politics, some readers or viewers would expect them also to be alternative by not being produced primarily to make a profit for their publishers, and by relying on participation and readership by average people rather than highly educated elites. Consumers of mainstream or right-wing activist media might not expect such a departure from typical business practices and goals.

The place of alternative media in culture

For those who accept the idea that alternative media is necessarily defined by its opposition to mainstream culture, a look at its past can be problematic. As Chapter 2 will explore in greater detail, there have been times when the banned and officially censored 'alternatives' have actually been more popular than mainstream, respectable media. At other times, activist and radical media have been very widely read and quite influential.

Like all forms of communication, alternative and activist media respond to the social situations they are produced in, including economic changes and overt or covert repression. At all times they provide a counter-narrative to that put forward by mainstream media, but that narrative can be expressed in many different ways, depending on the era.

For example, the late 1940s and 1950s are generally seen as a repressed and repressive time in the United States. With McCarthyism and anti-communist blacklisting in full flow, overtly political publishers and broadcasters frequently found their efforts blocked. And yet a counter-narrative emerged in the form of 'Beat' literature and poetry, avant-garde jazz, and eventually rock and roll. This narrative embraced concern about racism and poverty, as well as America's romantic possibilities: the freedom of the open road, the possibility of white 'beatniks' and Blacks getting to know each other, and the pursuit of radical self-change through exploring Eastern mysticism, sexuality, drugs, and extremes of human experience. Because of the times, even works that were resolutely apolitical (such as Jack Kerouac's books) had political resonance with readers, while others (such as the poetry of Diane di Prima and Allen Ginsberg) were able to be explicitly political because their views were presented in the context of a literary form rather than a political tract.

In the early 1960s, the political elements emerging from this counter-culture came to the fore, but its sociocultural elements receded or changed. One reason is that countercultural images are easily absorbed by mainstream culture, rendering them harmless. For the Beat sub-culture, this process included the use of the beatnik as a figure of fun in the popular media: for example, the suburban 'wannabe beatnik' Maynard G. Krebs portrayed on the sit-com *The Many Loves of Dobie Gillis* from 1959 to 1963. Once a subcultural or oppositional stance is established as something amusing, it's hard to see it as a threat.

This process, which is explored in greater detail in Chapter 9, has dogged the steps of alternative media as well as the subcultures from which it often emerges, from the adoption of popular features from radical papers by mainstream rivals to the increased use of colour and 'hip' design elements by mainstream magazines emulating the underground press of the 1960s. In 1977, only punk fanzines used 'ransom note'-style mixes of lettering styles; today this design note has become a hackneyed cliché found in advertisements for designer clothing and teen pop-music magazine layouts.

Suffice it to say that *form alone* is alternative only for a short while, and that expressions of subcultural resistance also exist in moments in time, beyond which they can devolve into self-parody. Content, intention, and production will, by necessity, evolve to fit the situation in which media is produced, or it will lose its relevance. Accordingly, alternative media are 'alternative' only in the context of their response to, and participation in, the cultures within which they are produced and consumed.

Travellers' Rest: a case to consider

Seven years ago Richard Waters started a web site to share some of his fiction, poetry, and essays, calling it Travellers' Rest. He is from an Irish Traveller background ('Irish Traveller' is a term used to indicate indigenous nomadic people in Ireland, or their relations who have moved abroad), so some of what he posted had to do with that interest. Waters didn't think of this as a political project – it was, at first, merely a way to share some reminiscences with whoever might be interested.

His audience changed his plans. 'The e-mails began to arrive, mostly from Country [settled] people who were intrigued by the affection and respect I expressed for a way of life that seemed to have been monstrously mutated over the intervening period, judging from the standard "news" sources available to them,' he explains:

> Some were from academics and students pursuing knowledge (or chasing 'paper'). Merely the correspondence about Travellers that I have felt the need to save, including my responses, totals almost 4000 messages; there have been many more over the last seven years. Somewhat surprisingly (to me, at least) there have also been an additional 1500 significant messages to and from Travelling People over that same period. All but a very few in each category have been quite supportive. Many solicited commentary from me concerning contemporary events involving Travellers, which in most cases quickly evolved into a critique of the conventional media treatment of those events.

And so it happened that Waters found himself approached by reporters, outsiders, and Travellers alike, all seeking comment on negative coverage of the Irish Traveller community in the US press. Waters refuses media interviews, declining to be seen as some sort of 'spokesman for Travellers'. He does post information about badly written articles, slanted broadcasts, and a selection of the emails he receives about them, along with his own answers. This material is 'intended to serve as additional background for interested parties to use in making their own decisions. I suppose one could call it an "alternative news" source', he says, 'an additional source to supplement, if not offset, the often biased, unsubstantiated coverage of Travellers by conventional sources'.

...

He maintains and updates Travellers' Rest alone, and pays all the costs for it out of his own pocket.

The site serves two audiences, Waters says: Irish Travellers themselves, and those who want to know more about them. He says he has a 'great relationship' with both, crafting his content mix in response to their enquiries.[11]

Travellers' Rest was not intended to become an activist publication, but it did so by default, at the behest of its readership. It serves an audience ignored by the mainstream press, and is not a business per se. Using the criteria explored so far, it would seem to be both 'alternative' and 'activist'.

Who needs an alternative?

This chapter's title posed the question: who needs an alternative? Considering the state of the mass media, perhaps we all do.

In a 2004 broadside titled 'The state of the media union', media critic Norman Solomon said: 'Television provides a wide variety of homogenized offerings. With truly impressive (production) values, the major networks embody a consummate multiplicity of sameness, with truncated imagination and consolidated ownership. These days, there's a captivatingly unadventurous cable channel for virtually every niche market.'[12]

If, as some researchers have argued, most people depend on the mass media to provide a link with society in general,[13] a huge number of media consumers are certain to feel let down – or worse – on a regular basis. As Solomon noted, even as the mass media appears to cater to a wider audience than ever, it offers a very narrow spectrum of views and content. Diverse readers and viewers are valued primarily as 'niche markets' at whom specifically tailored advertisements can be targeted.

Research appears to indicate that the more marginalised a population is, the more likely its members are to be dissatisfied with the mass media. For example, a 1998 survey of Native American media consumers found that 60 per cent were not satisfied with TV programmes aimed at adults, and over half were dissatisfied with children's programming. Reasons cited included negative and/or inaccurate portrayals of Native Americans – and many viewers said that their response was to turn off the box, seeking news and entertainment from tribal papers and other alternative sources.[14]

Socially marginalised or dissenting groups, subcultures, ethnic minorities, and others who inhabit liminal spaces in mainstream cultures may be most likely to seek out alternative media, and to create their own if it is not found. In a world where the mass media exist less to inform or entertain than to sell audiences to advertisers, these people's desires are unlikely to be met in the mainstream marketplace.

Those who work in the media can frequently be found muttering angrily around the water-cooler as well. They find that their scope for creativity and opinion is increasingly constrained by owners who demand standardised products aimed at standardised audiences.

'We're not in the business of providing news and information. We're not in the business of providing well-researched music. We're simply in the business of selling our customers products.'[15] That's a direct quote from the CEO of Clear Channel Communications Inc., the largest operator of radio stations in the US. When media bosses make comments like that, it should come as no surprise that many who entered the industry to inform or entertain want to find an alternative. But that will mean doing more than just pursuing new audiences and content – they'll have to alter the means of production itself to change the motive for publishing.

As the story of Traveller's Rest indicates, alternative media can have many different functions. For some, these alternatives will become their main source of information; for others, like Waters's readers, they are an enjoyable or provocative 'extra ingredient' in a mostly mass-media diet. Some alternative media will also be activist, offering a call to action, and some activist media may enter the mainstream and cease to be alternative. Still others will act as a vehicle for communication, self-enhancement, contemplation, or escape. And some will do all of these things at different times, in response to audience demand, outside events, or the interests of writers, videographers, researchers, artists, or publishers.

Exercises

1.1 A discussion of Albert's model programme for an 'alternative' media organisation

Read the following summary of Michael Albert's prescription for alternative media, and discuss it in the context of what you know, or think you know, about how mainstream media organisations work.

Albert's vision of a truly 'alternative' media is based on the concept of participatory economics, in which products (including media products) would be created and distributed by the people who make them, in the form of democratic workers' councils. That's not everyone's cup of tea, so naturally his proposals are controversial and provocative. Here's a summary of Albert's six suggestions for changing the means of production in the world of alternative media:[16]

1. People working in an alternative media organisation should earn the same amount of income for the same amount of work, regardless of job title. If there is a need for someone to be paid more (for example, if typical salaries for Web designers in your area are so high that you can't get anyone to work for what you're offering), there should be very clear reasons for them. Extra pay should not equal extra power in the organisation, however.

2. Decision-making should involve everyone who works in the organisation, and be as democratic as possible rather than hierarchical. People should have access to all the information they need to find out about what's at stake before they make a decision, and should be encouraged and supported to make their views known in an effective way.

3. Divisions of labour along the lines of gender and race should be diminished, even if that's difficult to do. Alternative media organisations should 'embody feminist and multicultural aims'.[17]

4. Whenever the alternative media organisation interacts with its audience, either in the product itself or in business relationships, these interactions should be based on these same internal values.

5. Alternative media organisations should try to appeal to broad, inclusive audiences – not just the advertisers' dream audience of upwardly mobile, affluent consumers.

6. Alternative media organisations should help each other, offering guidance, support, and practical assistance.

Answer these questions, in the context of an in-class discussion:

1. What advantages and disadvantages would media organisations adhering to these principles find?

2. Can you imagine yourself working for such an organisation? What do you think it would be like, and how would that experience differ from working at a traditional media organisation?

3. Would this business model necessarily result in a different end product than one employing the same individuals, but with a hierarchical decision-making process and a clear profit motive?

1.2 Is it alternative, activist, or both?

For this exercise, divide into four groups, each with use of a computer that has internet access. Meet with your group for 30 minutes to have a look at one of the following publications online. Each of these makes a claim to be alternative and/or activist. Consider that publication in reference to the definitions of alternative and activist media discussed in this chapter. Make a decision: does it qualify as one or both, and by whose criteria? Write down your decision and the reasons for it to share with the rest of the class, along with a description of the publication you've viewed.

On your return to class, discuss these publications and definitions, with reference to other media products that you are familiar with.

CASE STUDY GROUP 1: *THE SHINBONE* (WEB SITE)

The Shinbone is an online newsletter written, edited, and published by one person: Daniel Clark. Based in the US, it espouses conservative values, and takes a strict Constitutionalist approach to US politics. Typical articles discuss political developments from a right-wing perspective, with a particular focus on opposition to abortion. Although it carries a great deal of comment and opinion, the editor says:

> I think I would only consider *The Shinbone* to be activist insofar as it is an outlet for my own activism. I finally decided to create a site after I'd put a lot of work into an article on embryonic stem cell research, and I didn't want it to go to waste. Instead of waiting for ten weeks for some editor to reject it, I decided to become my own editor, although I didn't really know what I was getting myself into.

'*The Shinbone* is not a commercial site, so I'm not making a cent from it,' Clark adds. 'However, part of the site's purpose is to compile a body of work that will help me obtain a writing job at some point in the future.'[18]

Have a look at the latest edition at shinbone.home.att.net/main.htm

CASE STUDY GROUP 2: *RED PEPPER* (MAGAZINE AND WEB SITE)

Red Pepper is a left-Green magazine in the UK. It was started via a fundraising drive, and is run by a board that includes representatives from its editorial staff, its investors, and the left-Labourite Socialist Movement organisation ('to protect the integrity of the Charter against, for instance, the takeover of the company by some opportunistic shark with an eye for profitable left-wing magazines').[19]

It uses what one observer has called a 'commercial publishing model', with a concrete business plan, both paid and volunteer staff, and a relatively broad target audience. It relies on subscriptions, bookshop sales, some advertising, and shares purchased by supporters.[20]

Much of the print version's content, along with web links and other online-only items, is available at www.redpepper.org.uk.

CASE STUDY GROUP 3: *ASIANWEEK* (NEWSPAPER AND WEB SITE)
AsianWeek is the top English-language publication for the growing Asian market in the US. It has a circulation of 50,000 and about three times that many readers. It's distributed for free in the San Francisco Bay Area, where it reaches over 70 per cent of Asian-Pacific residents, and has many subscribers outside that area. Founded in 1979, it is published by a profitable family-run company started by Chinese-American journalist John Fang. The Fang company also owns the *Independent* freesheet, and for a time ran one of the city's two major daily papers, the *San Francisco Examiner*.

Have a look at the current issue of *AsianWeek* online at www.asianweek.com

CASE STUDY GROUP 4: *GREEN LEFT WEEKLY* (MAGAZINE, ARCHIVED ONLINE)
This weekly left-environmentalist publication from Australia is available in print and online. It was launched by the Democratic Socialist Party, has a staff of about six people, and is distributed primarily through subscriptions, left-wing bookshops, and street sales. Lead stories in *Green Left Weekly* usually cover political issues in Australia, but it also runs quite a bit of international news, opinion, and comment.

The latest issue and the magazine's archives are online at www.greenleft.org.au/index.htm

Further reading

The following sources look at the alternative press from a variety of different angles, covering why it is needed, how it is (or should be) run, and what is out there.

Abel, R. (1997) 'An alternative press: why?', *Publishing Research Quarterly*, 12 (4), 78–84.
Albert, M. (2003) *ParEcon: Life After Capitalism*. London: Verso Books.
Alliance for Community Media: www.alliancecm.org
Alternative Press Center/Independent Press Association – the Alternative Press Centre's Online Directory: www.altpress.org/direct.html
Alternative Press Review: www.altpr.org
Association of Independent Video and Filmmakers: www.aivf.org
    Includes online version of the *Independent* magazine.

Atton, C. (1999) 'A reassessment of the alternative press', *Media, Culture & Society*, 21 (1), 51–76.

Comedia (1984) 'The alternative press: the development of underdevelopment,' *Media, Culture & Society*, 6, 95–102.

NewPages: Alternatives in Print & Media: www.newpages.com

Phillips, P. (ed.) (2003) *Project Censored Guide to Independent Media and Activism*. New York: Seven Stories Press.

Radio4All: www.radio4all.org

Tsang, D. (2004) 'Traversing the alternative Web'. Online at sun3.lib.uci.edu/~dtsang/ttaw.htm (accessed 11 October 2004).

2 A brief history of alternative and activist media

An argument can be made that the history of alternative and activist media is as long as the history of media in general: for every official proclamation there has been a raucous popular ballad poking fun at the king. Indeed, print media in the West was seen as a challenge to the status quo from its very beginning. Printing press inventor Johann Gutenburg's first commercial printing projects in the 1400s were for official sponsors, but the Bibles that made him famous gave non-clerics access to information not previously available to the public. When the first newspapers appeared in Europe, they provided information on shipping, banking, conflicts, and current ideas to the emerging business class. This information had heretofore been strictly for the hereditary aristocracy and their trusted employees.

Knowledge is power, as a saying that originated on the masthead of a radical paper goes, and media have the ability to spread that power. This redistribution of power is not always a democratising process, however. An examination of the history of media reveals that each time media begin to reach or be made by a broader class or a marginalised sub-culture, a corresponding reaction can be expected from those currently in power. Media created by and for the working class appear to provoke the greatest reaction, with the possible exception of media seen as blasphemous by the dominant religious group of its day.

The example of the English radical press, which thrived in the early to mid-nineteenth century, is instructive. The availability of relatively inexpensive printing equipment and the expertise to run it coincided with the spread of radical ideas on labour, religion, and human rights. This combination fed an explosion of broadsheets, flyers, pamphlets, and newspapers that challenged the status quo. Papers bearing names like the *Poor Man's Guardian*, the *Free Inquirer*, and the *People's Paper* became tremendously popular. These carried a mixture of calls for social reform and entertaining writing about crimes and scandals. For example, the *Poor Man's Guardian* ran articles advocating workers' rights alongside song lyrics that drove the point home.[1]

The British government reacted by slapping taxes on paper, requiring licences to publish, and harassing publishers. Print shops were raided, equipment destroyed, and publishers jailed (for example, 68-year-old Peter Annet, the publisher of the *Free Inquirer*, was pilloried and jailed for writing about atheism).[2] But these actions failed to stop the radical press, which seemed to become even more powerful as official opposition increased.

Paradoxically, it was the relaxation of the 'taxes on knowledge' and other restrictive laws that led to the radical press's demise. These laws affected mainstream, respectable publications as well, to the chagrin of their publishers. Publishers of these papers written for an elite audience led the drive for increased freedom of the press, the achievement of which immediately lowered their production costs. They were also savvy enough to borrow some of the more popular features of the radical press, such as crime reports and gossip columns, to make their previously somewhat staid papers appeal to a wider audience. Advertisers, who sought the respectability by association and more affluent audiences that the mainstream papers could offer, flocked to these revamped publications. Armed with the financial backing to put out better-looking papers at competitive prices and to distribute them widely, the mainstream papers put their radical competitors out of business.

The emergence of codified news values

While the radical press was written and published by a large cast of amateurs and a few politically motivated professionals, this new popular press was professional all the way: papers were produced in a business environment, with profit as the primary goal. They were owned by wealthy individuals, or in some cases family firms, and owners frequently used their newspapers to put forward personal views on politics, social issues, and the like. It should be noted that these personal views did not always achieve primacy over those of editors, however, as an expectation of editorial independence could occasionally be invoked in the face of unwelcome demands from owners.

Indeed, newsrooms have always been the site of contentious arguments about what stories should run and how issues should be covered. Legal restrictions, express commands from owners and editors, and the interests of reporters all play a part in the creation of 'news values'. News values are the criteria by which those creating media decide whether a certain piece of information is newsworthy or not – obviously, even modern 24-hour rolling news operations like CNN cannot possibly report every event in the world.

David Randall provides a definition of news that expresses commonly held news values succinctly: 'the fresh, unpublished, unusual and generally interesting'.[3] But as he goes on to write, while the fresh and the unusual are relatively easy to identify, it isn't always simple to make a case that a story is interesting:

> There is no escaping subjectivity in judging news stories. It pervades the whole process of journalism and no reporter or news editor, try as they might professionally to suppress their own prejudices, will ever be able to do so completely. This is most obvious when they judge the basic story subject. I think homelessness is interesting and important, you think it is inevitable and boring. Such subjectivity ... is an ever-present danger, especially when journalists (often news editors) try to pass off their personal prejudices as objectivity.[4]

Like the personal prejudices of individual actors in the news-writing and editing process, the ideologies inherent in Western capitalism are also embedded in newsroom practices. The two combine to create the news values that mainstream papers abide by. It is these news values that determine which stories are covered, which sources are approached for information, and which points of view are privileged within the accounts that actually appear. In any culture and era, 'man bites dog' will probably always be a more interesting story than 'dog bites man'. But only under the news values that prevail in mainstream newsrooms is the impact of a strike on a few factory owners more interesting than the many workers' reasons for striking, or the earnings of a large company more important than the frustrations thousands of consumers may be encountering with its products.

The impact of market research and advertisements

Personal, social, and class prejudices and preferences played a role in the codification of news values from the start, but as the twentieth century began, owners and editors brought a new contributor into the newsroom debate: market research. Practitioners of this nascent 'science' were brought in to analyse media readership and content, with the primary purpose of changing the product to sell more papers and more advertisements. Newspapers, and successive media creations such as magazines, radio, film, and television, rapidly became part of a business-centred system in which 'reader', 'listener', and 'viewer' were just another set of synonyms for 'consumer'.

The newspapers' market researchers focused (and focus) on readers as both newspaper buyers and potential purchasers of products that advertisers would pay to showcase on the newspapers' pages. As advertising revenue outstripped income from per-copy sales, the pursuit of advertisers (and particularly those firms willing to pay the highest rates for ad space) became the primary focus of the market researchers' work. It would be foolish to assume that this research would not change news values, and indeed, its impact has long been blindingly obvious.

In 1944, the German philosopher Theodor Adorno, along with Max Horkheimer, was one of the first to issue a highly informed and withering critique of how what he called 'the culture industry' was permeated and perverted by its reliance on advertising. 'Advertising today is a negative principle, a blocking device: everything that does not bear its stamp is economically suspect,' he wrote. 'Because the system obliges every product to use advertising, it has permeated the idiom – the "style" – of the culture industry.' Advertising controlled not only what was presented, Adorno said, but how it was presented, with advertising and editorial barely distinguishable in the end.[5] While Adorno didn't live to see the ultimate fusion of advertising and editorial in today's branded television shows, logo-strewn clothing, and 'advertorial' magazine copy, his words were certainly prescient.

All mass media now make use of market research when planning the content and design of their products. Many have large in-house market research departments, and others have purchased or merged with major players in this industry.

Noam Chomsky, one of today's most influential critics of the mass media, offers up the demise of the British radical press as a prime example of how the market (pressures from advertisers and from countering competing products in the marketplace) has exerted a far more powerful influence on media content than governments ever could. While governments can choose to restrict or permit the business activities of publishers, Chomsky argues, economic factors underlie the majority of decisions and practices involved in producing media. These factors act as 'filters' that restrict its content. (Chomsky lists several other filters in his 'propaganda model' of the mass media, and interested readers are invited to explore his work for a more complete picture.)[6]

To start with, there is the cost of media-production equipment and the personnel needed to run it. Then there's the issue of competitiveness, on which the old British radical press foundered: once its products couldn't compete with mainstream papers on price and entertainment value, and once their competitors could get a better 'look' by investing in the latest printing presses with the money they got from advertisers, the radical press was effectively scuppered. Potential readers voted with their wallets.

Chomsky posits that this process has continued, and has intensified in the twenty-first century, because the start-up and running costs for mass media have increased exponentially. This makes launching and running competitive alternatives, whether print or broadcast, prohibitive. He says that to raise the needed cash, media must pander to advertisers or attract wealthy investors – or both. In either case, their involvement at the start of the media project will inevitably influence content to an even greater extent than it would if the publication's direction was already established before such influence came to bear.

This argument is demonstrably true, if one is looking at the alternative press as being primarily an alternative to the mass media. Selling a gourmet hamburger, or a veggie-burger, as an alternative to McDonald's burgers doesn't really create a huge difference in the food system: you're still selling a hamburger, and taking money in return. The compromises necessary to compete in a mass market, if one attempts to beat the mainstream media at its own game, as Comedia suggested (see Chapter 1), will eventually dilute the ideals that originally drove one's publishing plans.

For example, the left-of-centre *Guardian* newspaper in the UK was once known as a crusading daily published by middle-class liberals and aimed at a broad middle- and working-class audience.[7] Today, its glossy supplements and special sections are written to appeal to a middle- and upper-class audience, with features on designer fashions, expensive restaurants, sports cars, and exotic holidays. This content is seen as necessary to attract advertisers willing to pay the sorts of rates needed to keep a daily paper afloat in the modern age. Although critical views still appear in the *Guardian*, they may be counteracted by content elsewhere in the same publication: for example, an opinion piece decrying the environmental impact of increased air travel may well appear in the same issue as a travel supplement touting the pleasures of increased air travel, and a business-section story on how increased air travel is crucial to the British economy. This dissonance has a tendency to dilute the impact of those critical views that do emerge.

The philosopher Jürgen Habermas is well known for his critique of mass media, which he accuses of playing a major role in the atomisation of what he calls the 'public sphere'. He defines this as the public arena or arenas for reasoned debate between private individuals. Although today's mass media may seem to carry public debates, he argued, what it really does is manufacture a structured dialogue in which the 'winner' is always predetermined.[8] Chomsky has called this process 'manufacturing consent', in his book of the same name.[9]

Habermas acknowledged that alternative media might exist, but drew on the previous work of Adorno to criticise the 'culture industry' itself as a major actor in the destruction of the public sphere. Habermas's early writings concentrated on the middle-class public sphere, where free discourse between (primarily) educated white male individuals resulted in lively debates. Communication in this environment (the eighteenth-century British coffeehouse, for example, where early newsbooks and pamphlets were read and discussed) was horizontal – between equals – and generally unconstrained. Habermas argued that it was this en-vironment that allowed the emergence of democratic ideals, eventually leading to more democratic forms of government taking the place of hereditary monarchies.

Numerous critics have noted that the great majority of the population were excluded from this bourgeois public sphere,[10] and Habermas himself eventually adapted his theories to include working-class culture as an alternative public sphere.[11] In doing so, he raised the possibility of alternative media that act to support new groupings, providing infor-mation that can be discussed, or a mediated forum for such discussion. As John Downey and Natalie Fenton write:

> Habermas recognises not only the existence of alternative public spheres but also their capacity for challenging domination. While he maintains that his analysis of the public sphere infrastructure still pertains to a mass media largely subordinate to the interests of capital on the one hand, and the state on the other, he has in the mean-time revised his pessimistic opinion of the public. Rather than seeing the public as cultural dupes in the manner of Adorno and Horkheimer, he now emphasises the pluralistic, internally mass differentiated mass public ... that is able to resist mass-mediated representations of society and create its own political interventions.[12]

This formulation is closer to the concepts of hegemony and counter-hegemony espoused by theoretician Antonio Gramsci. Gramsci argued against earlier Marxist theories that saw class divisions and power relationships as created and cemented primarily by physical force and state power, saying that the dissemination and acceptance of ideologies espoused by the ruling elite were also necessary for the survival of hierarchical systems. At times, ideology might be imposed by force or threat – for example, when states mandate loyalty oaths, pledges of allegiance, or party membership. But most of the time, he noted, ideol-ogies are woven so tightly into public and private institutions that people generally see them as 'common sense' rather than an imposed system of beliefs.[13] When this occurs, these ideologies have become *hegemonic*: they are so embedded in a culture that they predominate over others. Efforts at countering them can be called *counter-hegemonic*.

Downey and Fenton write that one can understand the public sphere as an ever-changing entity made up of many overlapping discussions, not a single, static forum. While mass media may dominate, other conversations are going on, and may emerge into the mass-media forum during periods of change and crisis. Activism and advocacy of specific causes can deliberately create moments of rupture and transformation. The emergence of new communication technologies can also open up fresh spaces for dialogue.[14]

Technology and alternative media

Historically, whenever a new technology makes the creation of media less expensive rather than more so, that has a positive effect on the creation of alternative media. Just as the availability of relatively inexpensive printing presses that could be run by a single individual contributed to the rise of the radical press in nineteenth-century England, so the recent availability of consumer-priced video cameras has led to a rise in alternative videography (see Chapter 5). For example, trade unions and Catholic church groups in Brazil have taken advantage of recent developments by distributing low-cost video equipment to citizens' action groups around the country. These groups have then contributed footage on environmental disputes, union actions, and land ownership issues to video news compilations. The videotapes are widely distributed through a 'national popular video association'. The cost of production is minimal, and an ad-hoc distribution network has been developed that piggy-backs on existing church and union infrastructure for transportation, requiring nothing fancier than a TV and VCR at the point of delivery.[15]

Fax machines – ubiquitous in modern offices – were famously used by pro-democracy protesters in China to spread the word of arrests and actions in 1989. Their employment by alternative newspapers in Russia during Yeltsin's crackdown following the failed 1991 coup attempt is less well known.[16] When government agents shut down their presses, papers like the *Moscow Times* sent their information out by fax,[17] encouraging recipients to use the office copier to print up copies to distribute them further, and to fax them on to friends. People close to the scene of the action in Russian cities used faxes to get the word out. 'Our old fax-apparatus was hot, our fax-paper supply was running out. We feared most of all that our only computer would break down because of the tension!' writes one news agency employee who was working in St

Petersburg at the time.[18] With international networks like CNN blocked and national stations showing only re-runs of old films during the coup attempt, faxes and the RelCom computer network, which maintained links with the internet via email, became not alternative but essential.[19]

Perhaps the most recent technology to play a role in alternative media is the mobile telephone. From reform groups in Thailand during a 1992 uprising[20] to ethnic-minority truckers on strike in California in 2004,[21] the low cost and portability of mobile phones have turned them into a particularly potent media tool. Far-flung reporters can use them to call in copy, and with the latest models sporting still or video cameras, new possibilities are appearing.

Back to the future?

Some observers argue that in many ways, media in the early years of the twenty-first century looks very much as it did in the seventeenth century. Mass-media companies control almost all print and broadcast media, as well as mainstream news media online. Their level of control of content and access is analogous to that of governments 300 years ago. But as they did in the past with the advent of low-cost printing, new technologies may be opening the way for media forms that offer an alternative. Like the first publications to appear outside the realm of government approval (the *corantos*, newsbooks, and other unofficial compendiums of news of seventeenth-century Europe), these alternatives rely on low production costs to ensure viability, utilise new distribution networks, and have a highly personal flavour. Newsbooks were notable for their reliance on personal essays, and for utilising an editorial voice that addressed the reader directly. The 'citizen reporter' trend becoming evident in environments as distinct as Asian countries with hidebound, ultra-traditional mainstream media and the freewheeling American blogosphere has a very similar flavour.

Media theorist Chris Atton suggests that an inclusive model of alternative media should include all (or almost all) forms of media that are non-commercial, 'grassroots', or highly personal, such as blogs and fanzines, as well as somewhat more commercial publications that are predicated on citizen participation and contribute to furthering open debate.[22] Clemencia Rodríguez provides well-researched examples of the most inclusive efforts, which may be financed by unions and other social organisations. She indicates that these alternative media efforts, which she calls 'citizens' media', should not be compared with or expected to supersede mass media, but notes that they may have an impact far greater than their size and reach indicate.[23]

In Japan and Korea, non-journalists are using mobile phones, cheap video equipment, and the internet to feed information to new online alternative papers. Although Japan's *JanJan* (www.janjan.jp) and Korea's *OhmyNews* (www.ohmynews.com) are published by small companies that hope to turn a profit, their use of non-professional, and often activist, contributors means that they cover very different stories from their mainstream competitors. For example, *OhmyNews* recently ran a story revealing the high level of suicide amongst Korean students due to college exam pressure, kicking off a firestorm of comment that eventually reached the national media. It has gained a level of popularity unimaginable for most 'alternative' newspapers, with about 750,000 daily readers for the online edition and now a successful weekly print edition as well. Over two-thirds of all households in Korea have an internet connection, and internet cafés are ubiquitous on its cities' high streets, so an online delivery system isn't the barrier to readership that it might be elsewhere.[24]

At *JanJan*, writer Masuru Yamamuru says he contributes to the alternative daily because mainstream papers in Japan rely too closely on government press releases and corporate advertorial.[25] By working as individual freelancers, but with the assistance of *JanJan*'s small fact-checking and editorial staff, reporters like Yamamuru can investigate stories that are below the radar of the mass media, and write them in highly personal language that appeals to readers. These publications have made the idea of 'citizens' media' commercially viable, and their success indicates that even within the larger mass media arena there is a demand for a counter-hegemonic effort.

Many media critics see such successes as heartening, but they are not unproblematic. Cable systems with 400 channels to choose from, and the internet with its billions of web sites, can be seen as 'citizens' media' simply because so many voices can be heard through them, but they are also organised in ways that allow people to avoid those views that do not coincide with their own. Self-segregation can potentially lead to increased polarisation rather than increased discourse, and recent research indicates that both processes are in play.[26] Unlike readers of a newspaper such as *JanJan*, who can read articles from different viewpoints and also see extensive online feedback on them, it is possible for cable viewers and selective web users to remain in an 'information ghetto', encountering only views that mirror their own.

Hans Enzensberger suggests that an alternative media with the greatest potential to re-form the public sphere would be one in which media creators and media audiences communicate horizontally – and in some forms of alternative media, such as fanzines, creators and audiences may well be one and the same. Such democratic forms would take as their subjects the issues ordinary people face, rather than the consumption of luxury goods or the spectacles of Hollywood. They would exist to serve the public's need for information, and be informed by the public rather than by advertisers, oligarchs, or governments.[27]

Can such media be created and kept going in today's 'mass-mediated' world? Is it possible that they could develop the ability to inform and move populations, as the British radical press once did? It's hard to answer these questions – only time (and hard work on the part of alternative and activist media practitioners) will tell.

Certainly, there is a wide consensus among critics of the mass media that it serves the public poorly. An additional problem is that the mass media is now dominated by a few very large corporations. Such entities can amass vast political power, including the power to get laws rewritten in their favour. Like the 'respectable' publishers of eighteenth-century Britain, they have access to the top ranks of government. They can arrange for controls to be imposed or lifted according to which sort will benefit themselves most, or in order to harm competitors. The world's top media corporations have a near-monopoly on the dissemination of news and other information. It is not paranoid to worry about the impact of this monopoly on public discourse and civil society, should alternative voices be deliberately silenced.

This book attempts to put current alternative media in perspective, and in context. Efforts to analyse the media that look only at mainstream offerings run the risk of missing or underplaying the importance of counter-hegemonic efforts; it may also be true that some examinations of alternative media read too much into them. The only certainty is that alternative media emerge and persist in all eras, in all political systems, and for a wide variety of reasons.

The following chapters will examine alternative media practices and products, and encourage the applications of lessons drawn from both history and theory to the creation of future alternatives.

Exercises

2.1 Media ownership and business models in history

You could examine the history of almost any major media corporation to see the trends described in this chapter in action. The Thomson Corp., a publicly traded, multinational media corporation that began its life as a Canadian newspaper owned by a single individual, provides a well-researched corporate history, including an interactive timeline, at www.thomson.com/corp/about/ab_history.jsp. Which changes in media ownership and business models are illustrated in this history? How might these changes have affected prevalent news values amongst the staff of Thomson's media products?

2.2 Media ownership and news values

Working in small groups, choose a major newspaper, such as *The Times* or the *Washington Post*, or a major broadcasting company, such as CNN, NBC, or Star Television. Use reference books and the web to find out about its owners and their links to other corporations. Seek out information on its news values – most major media companies publish a 'mission statement' that encapsulates their stated news values; alternatively, examine one or more issues or broadcasts and come to your own conclusions. Compare these findings with any critical opinions you can find, either online or in books like those listed in the 'Further reading' section below.

2.3 Media ownership, news values, and ideology at Fox News

View the film *Outfoxed*, a documentary on the Fox News Network produced and directed by Robert Greenwald. Discuss ways in which ideology informs Fox's news values, according to Greenwald. (If possible, draw on your own observations from watching Fox.) How does Fox transmit its ideology to viewers? How might its news values and ideologies be connected to its ownership? (The *Outfoxed* DVD and additional materials are available at www.outfoxed.org)

Further reading

Atton, C. (2002) *Alternative Media*. London: Sage.

Bagdikian, B. (2004) *The New Media Monopoly*. Boston: Beacon Press.

Chomsky, N. (2002) *Media Control: The Spectacular Achievements of Propaganda*. New York: Seven Stories Press.

Curran, J. and Gurevich, M. (eds) (2000) *Mass Media and Society*. London: Hodder Arnold.

Curran, J. and Seaton, J. (1991) *Power Without Responsibility: The Press and Broadcasting in Britain*. London: Routledge.

Downing, J. (1980) *The Media Machine*. London: Pluto Press.

Free Press (2004) *Media Reform News* and other electronic publications. Available at www.freepress.net (accessed 9 November 2004).

Herman, E. S. and Chomsky, N. (1988) *Manufacturing Consent: The Political Economy of the Mass Media*. New York: Random House.

McChesney, R. and Nichols, J. (2002) *Our Media, Not Theirs: The Democratic Struggle Against Corporate Media*. New York: Seven Stories Press.
Media Day Group JMK (2003) Media Day project site. Available at www.jmk.su.se/global03/project/mediaday/index.html (accessed 9 November 2004).

3 Unheard voices, unseen images

If the mass media address atomised audiences, or see their audiences as 'products' to be sold to advertisers, many alternative media attempt to bring people together. These productions are often (but not always) created by and for groups marginalised by 'race', gender, sexuality, disability, or beliefs. Whether it's about grassroots efforts at media creation by these groups, or attempts to create alternative media that service their own needs, this is one area where media access can be a crucial component of community inclusion, self-advocacy, and empowerment.

Matching media to audiences

Low cost and ease of access are the keys to success for people on the edge. For would-be producers, that means paying attention to whether or not the desired audiences can access their products, as well as to production costs and the skills available within the production group. For example, the web is very inexpensive to develop media for, but easy access to the internet is not yet a reality in most poor neighbourhoods, or amongst many minority groups. However, as the section on Autistics.org in this chapter will illustrate, there are marginal groups for whom online media are a preferred option.

Probably the most accessible form of media is radio. At least one person in ten has access to a radio, and the developing world is home to over 800 million radio receivers.[1] In Western Europe and North America, access is close to universal.[2]

As a format, radio can be received by anyone able to hear, whereas illiteracy and poor literacy limit access to both the web and print media. Radio is also relatively cheap to develop content for. Although quality may suffer, a hand-held tape recorder will suffice for basic tasks.

Print media also have advantages. Print is a familiar format to most people, and even those who are unable to read themselves can often find someone to read a document to them. That said, many people overesti-mate the level of literacy, both in their own community and in general. Current estimates indicate that in the UK and US, 20 per cent of the population is functionally illiterate;[3] in deprived communities the rate is generally higher; and in some parts of the developing world it can approach 90 per cent.

Even in these situations, however, print media can be used. For example, the World Association for Christian Communication, a religious organisation working to increase media access and reduce illiteracy in the developing world, uses calendars, billboards, stickers, and posters in a campaign to get children in India to enrol in school. It has also utilised a rickshaw with a cassette player and loudspeaker system, and street theatre performances.[4] This mixed-media approach makes particularly good sense when working with audiences that may have a variable literacy rate.

Although not everyone owns a TV set, video (or DVD) can also be a very accessible medium in certain circumstances. In India, for example, only about 25 per cent of households have a colour TV set[5] – most of these in urban areas. Far fewer have their own VCRs, DVD players, cable television, or satellite TV access. In rural areas, however (and in many urban apartment blocks as well), neighbourhood entrepreneurs will hook several homes up to a single VCR or satellite dish.[6] Videotapes, DVDs, or satellite broadcasts can also be shown to groups in schools, clinics, town halls, or private homes. Reproducing videotapes is very cheap, and with the advent of low-cost DVD burners, that technology looks likely to follow suit.

Recognising underserved audiences

It's not just the developing world where some people's voices are not heard. People with disabilities, people of colour, children, and poor people rarely influence the content of mass-media products. Journalists are unlikely to interview these people, and as a result, stories are rarely written specifically about how they will be affected by news develop-ments. They are also absent from or underrepresented in the workforces of mass-media organisations, Even women, who actually slightly out-number men in most places, receive less news coverage and are less likely to be employed in the media than men. For example, according to the American Journalism Survey carried out by the Indiana University School of Journalism in 2002, whilst more than 60 per cent of the people graduating with degrees in journalism are female, women hold only one-third of the full-time positions in journalism, and their numbers in the workforce are not increasing.[7] Other researchers have noted that female journalists are less likely than their male counterparts to be in editorial, managerial, or ownership positions, where they can have an impact on which stories are covered.[8]

Have a look around. Who is seen, interviewed, and covered in your own local, regional, and national media? Who is not? If you can, figure out why not ... and think about ways in which the situation could be remedied. If you are interested in alternative and/or activist media, these are the audiences – and the potential media producers – who are most likely to benefit from your work, and who have an obvious reason to want to get involved with it.

The following three sections profile alternative and/or activist media projects. These publications serve different audiences, involve varied groups of producers, are funded differently, and utilise quite a range of media.

A place for self-advocacy: Autistics.org

Autism is a spectrum of developmental differences that affects approximately 1 in 200 people. It is characterised by difficulties with social interaction, impaired verbal and non-verbal communication, and stereo-typical and repetitive interests and activities. There has been a great deal written about people with autism, but very little written by them about themselves. And because difficulties with social interaction and communication are part of the condition, it can be difficult for people with autism to make themselves heard in the mass media. Typically, when reporters cover a story about autism they interview the parents of autistic people, or professionals in autism services or research.

The web site Autistics.org (www.autistics.org) is one of the few media outlets trying to change this situation. It's run by a small group of people who have autism, including the founder, Laura Tisoncik. She describes it as 'a global database for information useful to ... controlled by ... [and] created by' people with autism.[9]

Tisoncik taught herself HTML, the coding language used to build web sites, some years ago. 'HTML was crude then, so it was easy to learn,' she says, noting that as it has become more complex she has increasingly relied on graphical editing software that allows the designer to choose options from a menu to build a web page. The actual coding goes on behind the scenes with these packages, making it relatively simple for even a novice to build a serviceable web site.

Funding used to be from the team's own pockets, but the site now receives small donations from individuals through PayPal, a system that allows people to send cash to others over the internet. 'In the past year donations have been just enough to cover the expenses so that I've not had to dip into my own pocket in any unplanned way,' Tisoncik says.

The main Autistics.org site acts as a host for several individual web sites, announcements of events and campaigns, links to articles of interest from the mainstream media, and commentary on media representations of autism, 'treatments' for the condition, and court cases.

Because mainstream media coverage of autism is biased towards seeing it as a disease-like condition that should be 'cured' or eradicated, Tisoncik notes, alternative points of view are rarely welcome outside of sites like Autistics.org. And since most of the organisations focused on autism are made up of parents and professionals, there are also few non-media outlets for discussion. 'We are systematically excluded from any serious role in determining autism policy, when in fact as the persons most directly affected we should have the *major* role,' she explains. 'We're systematically excluded from those services we need to live independently in favor of funding programs that are, really, all about advancing professional careers and/or placating parents.'

That situation frequently results in calls for letter-writing and more direct activism through lists and forums affiliated with or linked to Autistics.org. 'I hope we're one more step towards authentic autistic liberation,' Tisoncik says, 'meaning pretty much the same thing that it meant to liberate the slaves: to count us as full human beings, with all the rights and liberty and dignity that this indicates, and not as three-fifths of some non-profit organisation's puzzle logo.'[10]

The site has been the home of a long-running campaign to publicise the peculiar reaction that the all-too-frequent murder of an autistic child or adult by a parent or carer typically receives in the mass media: the parent or carer is often described as having 'snapped' due to stress, and is pitied or even excused rather than being prosecuted. Generally, little or no attention is paid to the murder victim's right to life, or to changing the intolerable social conditions that are said to have led to the crime. Autistics.org has also drawn attention to research aimed at prenatal identification of autism, and to the eugenicist measures that are likely to result from it, as has been the case with prenatal identification of Down syndrome.

The site acts as a distribution base for other, non-electronic forms of media, such as badges and posters.

Autistics.org serves a very specific audience, one with the collective experience of being silenced either by inability to communicate using speech or by the tendency of others not to listen to what they have to say. This type of alternative media project, whether it utilises print or other forms of media, tends to become activist, even if that was not the media creators' original intention. The community of people involved shape the media to fit their own needs at first, but once a critical mass of discussion occurs, it often erupts in other-directed activity.

The medium is not necessarily the message

Fanzines are small, self-produced magazines. They're usually a non-commercial venture, and can cover almost anything that those who make them find interesting – although music (especially punk rock) and science-fiction fandom are probably the biggest topics. (Fanzines are covered in greater detail in Chapter 7.)

When Justin Marler first encountered the fanzine world, it was in the context of punk underground publishing in the San Francisco Bay area. 'The zine world was considered a completely free zone for expression,' he says. 'Anyone could express absolutely anything they wanted and it was generally respected. This made it one of the most pure free speech forums around.'

For Marler, however, one thing that was missing was a discussion of spirituality, a topic that he was intensely interested in. He had spent some time in a Russian Orthodox monastery, to which he soon returned with his zine project. *Death to the World* was a unique item, even in a publishing world that was chock-a-block with quite diverse material. 'My exposure to punk and metal was the foundation for my design approach,' Marler explains. 'I coupled this edgy punk look with the more severe side of ancient religious art, and the result of this combination was a very appealing visual world. I saw many connections and similarities with the punk look and the ancient icons of martyrs.'

Although his zine looked similar to punk music zines, the content was a highly personal take on Marler's own ascetic quest for spiritual understanding, with contributions from others who were experiencing similar feelings about the emptiness of consumer culture, but had not found that ready-made subcultures like punk or the metal scene provided enough spiritual sustenance. 'The zine did muster up interest in Orthodox Christianity, but more importantly, it gave a lot of hope to a lot of people that were suffering and felt they were alone in their suffering,' he says. 'According to some of the letters I received, the zine gave hope to many people in prison, kids on the streets, drug addicts, abused young people, those with broken hearts, and even prevented someone from committing suicide. I'm very proud of *Death to the World* and what it meant.'

Like most zines, *Death to the World* was distributed in a few small shops, usually record stores, but in this case some Orthodox bookshops as well.

Figure 3.1 *Death to the World* fanzine used Russian Orthodox imagery in a publishing format more closely associated with underground music. (Photo: Mitzi Waltz)

Marler also traded copies with literally hundreds of other zine-makers. When he felt that the project had run its course – about the time that it began to receive interest from the mainstream press – he produced a final issue, and later had all of the issues made into a book. Small-press books can also be a form of alternative media.

Marler said his project was not intended as a way to proselytise (attract new members) for the Russian Orthodox group he was involved in. However, some alternative media may have exactly this kind of outreach in mind: for example, attracting people who might be interested in joining a political or cultural movement. Like *Death to the World*, however, some forms of alternative media can be primarily vehicles for self-expression, friendship, and mutual support. Also, any media format can be adapted to fit any purpose, according to the background and interest of the person or group creating it.[12]

Involving audiences, creating media creators

When government edicts on an epidemic of foot-and-mouth disease in 2001 forced mass slaughter of cattle and sheep in the English countryside, the mainstream media parachuted into villages around the country in search of soundbites and pictures full of pathos. When the story had run its course, they moved on – as usual.

'The media industry, especially broadcast and TV, have traditionally had a very fickle relationship with the countryside,' explains Nic Millington, director of the Hereford-based Rural Media Company (www.ruralmedia.co.uk). 'Every so often they would sort of beam down into a rural area when a particular issue was coming up on the agenda, but then leave very little behind them in the form of skills, renumeration or, indeed, accurate representation. They left a degree of disappointment in the communities that had participated in those programmes.'

The Rural Media Company focuses on working with marginalised rural audiences, particularly young people, enabling them to become media creators rather than the subject of occasional reports or passive media consumers. Its funding comes from a patchwork of government initiatives, foundations, and charitable groups such as Comic Relief.

'My main motivation for starting the Company was that I was aware at a very local level of a lot of good media/arts work going on, particularly with young people, using cameras and some new technology, but not really managing to reach wide audiences,' Millington says. 'The production values were such that they were not able to communicate very effectively.' The RMC was created to build a bridge between rural people and the media industry. The goal, Millington says, is 'enabling local people to use increasingly higher quality new technologies and to broker relationships between themselves, the industry, and groups that have professional or industrial skills'.

One of the RMC's latest projects is the online magazine *InSITE* (www.insitemag.net), a high-quality multimedia production utilising text, still photography, and audio and video clips. All of the material is by young people participating in RMC programmes. Millington describes it as a 'local democracy project' that 'challenges the ways in

Figure 3.2 *InSITE* is based in a shop-front office in Hereford, which also provides a location for young people's media workshops. (Photo: Rural Media Company)

which rhetoric about "youth participation" is being used in most public services delivery. We feel that young people's voice is still discouraged, [and] their opinions are not sought out or listened to. If young people can publish their own work publicly, you find that the education authority, teachers, parents, and so on will listen more carefully because it's in the public domain.'

Many of the teens and young adults who get involved with RMC have low literacy skills when it comes to written work, but what Millington calls their 'tele-literacy skills' – an in-depth understanding of narrative, characterisation and the like honed by watching hours of daytime television while bunking off school, in some cases – are strong. RMC gives them the advice and tools they need to build on these skills: 'by really putting the tools into their hands, we find they can speak the language well, and we can help them apply it,' Millington says.

Is what the RMC does a form of alternative media? Millington thinks so: 'It's alternative in the sense that we spend very little time trying to pitch proposals or get commissioned work from the mainstream media.' Some RMC productions, like a hard-hitting poster series on ethnic-minority youth in rural Britain and the eerie, supernatural-tinged film

The Vawn made by community film workshop participants in the Midlands village of Kington, may get mainstream press coverage. Some may even be granted a broadcast slot. However, they are mainly made by and for the communities they cover. The end goal, says Millington, is personal empowerment and social change.[13]

Who is unheard and unseen?

People can find themselves cut off from the mass media for many reasons: gender, sexuality, 'race', disability, political allegiance, religious belief – the list could go on. A group may be too small to attract attention, or too controversial to gain editorial approval.

Alternative media offer these audiences a way to communicate with each other, to provide information and support where it is needed, and to get involved in creating media that serves their own needs. When these projects take on an activist nature, they can bring the views of marginalised groups to the wider public, making media products that are advocates of and actors for change.

Exercises

3.1 Who is on the margins of the media?

Discuss the following questions, on the basis of this chapter, the readings listed, and your own personal knowledge:

1. What groups can you think of that have little or no access to the media in your area?
2. How about nationally – are there groups that are excluded or who have only limited access?
3. What factors can you identify in their marginalisation, in terms of both access to media creation and access as audiences to media that reflect their needs and interests?

3.2 Locked away from the media

Perhaps no group has more barriers to media access than those that our societies choose to confine in prisons and similar closed institutions. The following web sites provide information about the issues. Working in three groups, prepare a presentation on one of the following three topics:

1. Untold stories: media coverage of prisons and prisoners.
   Resources:
   Vosters, H. (1999) 'Media lockout: prisons and journalists', *MediaFile*, 18 (5). Available at www.media-alliance.org/mediafile/18-5/prisons.html (accessed 22 November 2004).
   Prison News Network (click on 'Issues'): www.vip-cali.com/pnn/default.htm
   Stamoulis, A. (2001) 'Prison policy in a media-driven America', *LiP Magazine*, August. Available at www.lipmagazine.org/articles/featstamoulis_126.shtml (accessed 22 November 2004).
2. Media created by prisoners.
   Resources:
   Prison Radio: www.prisonradio.org/front.html
   Journal of Prisoners on Prison (various issues). Published annually. Information and order forms for issues online at www.cspi.org/books/p/prisoners.htm
   Matthews, T. (2001) 'Editor in prison: Paul Wright talks about running a paper in prison', *Washington Free Press*, 49 (January/February). Online at www.washingtonfreepress.org/49/editor.html
   Prison Legal News: www.prisonlegalnews.org
3. Media access for prisoners/prisoners as media sources.
   Resources:
   Books to Prisoners Program: www.prisonbookprogram.org
   Kirby, K. (1999) 'Opening closed doors', *Communicator*, December. Online at www.rtndf.org/foi/ocd.html (accessed 22 November 2004).
   Sacramento, CA: Fight the Death Penalty (1997) 'Prisoners punish inmates because of "negative" news'. Available at www.fdp.dk/uk/cond/cond-09.htm (accessed 22 November 2004).
   McMullin, R. and Sussman, P. Y. (1996) 'Prison inmate's letter to a freelancer is first test of rigid new media rules', *NewsLink*. San Francisco: Society of Professional Journalists. Online at spj.org/norcal/link/prison_story.html (accessed 22 November 2004).

After each group has shared its findings, discuss what you've learned. Answer the following questions:

1. Why might it be important for media to have access to prisoners as news sources?
2. What do journalists need to be aware of, and careful about, when sourcing news within prisons?
3. How might alternative and activist media practitioners improve our knowledge of prisoners and prisons?

Further reading

Ainley, B. (1998) *Black Journalists, White Media*. Stoke on Trent: Trentham Books.

Alia, V. (2000) *Un/Covering the North: News, Media and Aboriginal People*. Vancouver, BC: University of British Columbia Press.

Asian Media Access: www.amamedia.org/ama/index.shtml

Barlow, W. (1998) *Voice Over: The Making of Black Radio*. Philadelphia: Temple University Press.

Brown, D. R. (1996) *Electronic Media and Indigenous Peoples: A Voice of Our Own?* Ames, IA: Iowa State University Press.

Coleman, R. M. (ed.) (2002) *Say It Loud! African American Audiences, Media, and Identity*. New York: Garland.

DeJong, W., Shaw, M., and Stammers, N. (2005) *Global Activism, Global Media*. London: Pluto Press.

Features on the US microradio movement: www.diymedia.net/feature/micro

Girard, B. (1999) 'Radio broadcasting and the internet: converging for development and democracy', *Voices* 3(3). Online at www.comunica.org/kl/girard.htm (accessed 17 November 2004).

Hartley, J. and McKee, A. (2000) *The Indigenous Public Sphere: The Reporting and Reception of Indigenous Issues in the Australian Media 1994–1997*. Oxford: Oxford University Press.

Lehrman, S. (1996) 'When it comes to diversity, newspapers don't walk the talk', *NewsLink*. San Francisco: Society for Professional Journalists. Available at spj.org/norcal/link/diversity.html (accessed 22 November 2004).

Media Awareness Network (Canadian organisation providing resources and support for media literacy and access for young people): www.media-awareness.ca/english/index.cfm

Murray, S. (2004) *Mixed Media: Feminist Presses and Publishing Politics*. London: Pluto Press.

Next 5 Minutes blog (documentation and discussion of tactical media projects): www.n5m4.org/journal5ef0.html?118

OurMedia/NuestrosMedias (global network of media activists and practitioners for alternative, activist, and community media): www.ourmedianet.org

Women's Institute for Freedom of the Press (includes an online directory of women's media projects): www.wifp.org

4 Anyone with a cheap transmitter can do radio

Radio receiver ownership is ubiquitous, transmission equipment can be inexpensive, and low literacy levels are no barrier to media production or consumption. Accordingly, radio may be the epitome of alternative media. This chapter uses several case studies to explore the use of radio by linguistic minorities, indigenous peoples, political dissenters, and subcultures. These will include community, minority and indigenous, and pirate radio.

Radio waves carry information that can be transmitted at particular frequencies. There is a limited spectrum of frequencies available, and international and national governments have made agreements that set aside various parts of this spectrum for different uses. For example, mobile phones operate on a certain range of frequencies, and radio-controlled toys use a different part of the spectrum. The kind of radio broadcasts you can receive with a regular, analogue radio use yet another range.

Depending on licensing laws where you live, and in some cases on the availability of community access schemes, digital radio technologies, and other factors, radio can still be a viable medium for non-mainstream producers and broadcasters. There are several different ways to get alternative and activist content on the air. The following sections explain how these work.

Using commercial networks

In urban areas, most of the frequencies on the radio broadcast dial have been licensed to existing radio stations. These licences can change hands for huge amounts of money, and are out of range for all but the most well-capitalised alternative media moguls. Air America (www.airamericaradio.com), a network of liberal stations set up to counter right-wing talk radio in the United States, represents a successful bid to provide alternative content via commercial radio. Air America doesn't own the stations that carry its broadcasts, but has instead contracted with a series of stations that were performing poorly in their areas. It splits advertising revenue with the station owners, which in the US are invariably large corporations like ClearChannel Communications.[1]

Air America has been capitalised by wealthy investors interested in promoting progressive politics.[2] The station currently develops all of its own programming, but similar stations elsewhere have been willing to take on programmes made by outside groups, either as one-off specials or as a regular part of their daily schedule. Despite its activist political mission, Air America is a commercial station, so its programming needs to have content and a level of quality that will attract enough listeners. Only if its audiences are sufficiently large will potential advertisers feel that their money will be well spent if they buy air time to promote their products. A group with access to media expertise and appropriate equipment could potentially provide this level of content – but it's a big job, and one that would require a large number of people to devote their labour to the project full-time.

Community-access radio

Some countries have set aside a small part of the radio spectrum for community access stations. These stations may receive public funds or be funded by a combination of grants and donations from listeners – in the US, where there are community stations in most major markets, the telethon-style 'pledge drive' is a familiar and annoying part of their annual broadcast schedules.

KPFA Radio (www.kpfa.org), based in the university town of Berkeley, California, was the first community-access station in the US, and typifies this type of broadcasting outlet. It first went on the air in 1949, and has since been funded through a combination of grants from private bodies like the Ford Foundation and local fundraising activities. It now has a few paid staff, but most of the people who work in KPFA's offices are volunteers. It is also the home of the Pacifica network, which provides alternative and activist radio shows to other community-access stations around the country.

A typical KPFA broadcasting day includes a mixture of music (the accent is on minority ethnic music and other music not found on commercial stations – folk, punk, hip-hop, and the like); current affairs shows; interviews with authors, politicians, economists, and other interesting thinkers; and news. Slots are set aside for programming by and about underrepresented groups, including women, youth, and people with disabilities. KPFA also offers 18-month apprenticeships to individuals from underrepresented groups.[3]

Licences for similar not-for-profit radio stations have only recently become available in the UK, following a long campaign by people who would like to set up an alternative radio sector.[4] Previously, non-commercial radio in the UK had been limited to small stations, most based in schools, universities, or hospitals, which were licensed to broadcast for only a small part of the day or year.

Low-power and micropower radio

Running a full-time station is not practical for many groups, and is certainly beyond the means of individuals. There is a small-scale, far less costly alternative, although its legality will vary according to where you live: low-power radio, and its even lower-power cousin, micropower broadcasting, or microradio.

Simply defined, micropower broadcasting involves transmitting at a very low level of power, usually 0.5 to 1 watt. This will provide radio coverage to a small area, perhaps one to three miles from the location of the transmitter. In densely populated urban environments, however, such broadcasters could reach quite large audiences.[5]

Low-power radio (also known as low-power FM, or LPFM) is the next step up, using an amplifier to bump transmission output to as high as 20 to 24 watts. This will extend the broadcasting range up to ten to fifteen miles from the transmitter, or even further under some circumstances.[6] As the level of watts gets higher, however, broadcasters run the risk of interfering with commercial radio signals. Licensing laws require avoiding this, and going through official licensing procedures, such as the US Federal Communications Commission's new LPFM licensing application process, may allow low-power stations to broadcast at up to 100 watts without causing problems to commercial neighbours on the radio dial.[7]

How far micropower and low-power transmissions will be received depends on your power output, the equipment you use – particularly the height and placement of your broadcasting antenna – and the terrain in your area. In a hilly city like San Francisco or Rome, an antenna placed high above the city would provide quite wide coverage, whilst one placed lower down would be blocked from reaching some areas by hills getting in the way.

The Radio4All web site listed at the end of this chapter provides a very thorough primer on the kind of equipment needed for both micropower and low-power radio. Licensing issues must be taken up with your country's airwaves regulator. In the US, this is the FCC (www.fcc.gov); in the UK, it's the Office of Communications, better known as Ofcom (www.ofcom.org.uk); and in Canada it's the Canadian Radio-television and Telecommunications Commission (www.crtc.gc.ca). Details of regulatory agencies in other areas can be obtained from the International Telecommunication Union (www.itu.int), an international organisation of government agencies and private-sector firms working in all sectors of licensed radio.

Pirate radio

Licensed, legal low-power radio is still thin on the ground in most areas. What can often be found is unlicensed, illegal low-power or microbroadcasting, better known as pirate radio.

At one time, there were high-power pirate stations operating across the US border in Mexico, and on ships just outside UK waters. These stations were hugely popular, commercial operations, offering rock and roll and youth culture at a time when the mainstream airwaves did not.

Today, however, the majority of pirate stations are small, fly-by-night operations involving just a few people and not reliant on traditional advertising. Most use the FM dial; others can be found on shortwave radio. The equipment used can fit in a suitcase. Indeed, a web search as this book went to press revealed a do-it-yourself guide to broadcasting using nothing more than an Apple iPod and a tiny wireless transmitter. The transmitter was intended by the manufacturer for making an iPod run through a car radio, but hackers found that it was adjustable to broadcast considerably further.[8] Unlicensed stations have broadcast from urban tower blocks, suburban bungalows, vans, even bicycles and backpacks.

In urban areas, small pirate stations can become incredibly popular. In London, for example, the house, garage, and grime music scenes have their roots deep in pirate radio. Upwards of sixty pirate stations were in operation in London as this book went to press, and pirate operators are credited with airing underground music that only later appears on commercial stations.

For example, the pirate station Delight 103 (website.lineone.net/~delightfm/home.htm) is closely associated with the So Solid Crew collective, which eventually hit the mainstream charts with the single 'They Don't Know'. The station grew out of a club night called 'Garage Delight', and was started in 1999 by local DJs and rap MCs, with assistance from a south London record shop, Unique Muzik. It takes advertisements, plays music, and has a regular group of DJs who have become 'local superstars'.

Stations like Delight 103 have been called a hotbed for new talent, and are widely credited with not only breaking new artists but also influencing mainstream radio playlists. As music critic Ian Youngs has written, these stations 'fill the gaps that out-of-touch legal stations ignore'.[9]

Digital radio

Most Western nations are in the process of rolling out digital radio, a new system that will allow twice as many stations to air on the FM band. Officially known as Digital Audio Broadcasting (DAB) radio, this system is basically just a technological upgrade to current analogue systems. On the transmission side, broadcasts are encoded as digital files. DAB receivers can decode these files, which will not be changed or ruined due to bad weather or bouncing off obstacles on their way. DAB radio receivers also have built-in technology that filters out interference, allowing radio stations to broadcast their signals closer together without overlapping.

Eventually, digital radio is slated to replace analogue radio, meaning that millions of existing radio receivers will have to be discarded and replaced.

The optimistic observer might say that expansion of the available bandwidth through high-tech changes should mean more room for community, minority, and alternative broadcasting to take its place alongside existing commercial stations. Sadly, it looks as though there is little hope of this prediction coming true: as Pete Tridish and Amy Mammersmith of the Prometheus Project have put it, 'because the transition to digital technology is being directed by a group of large stations and some of the biggest corporations involved in broadcasting, it is likely to result in only more of the same'.[10]

Commercial radio stations are already making profitable use of their regulator-assigned 'buffer zones' for running side businesses, such as chat and contest lines. The FCC and similar licensing agencies in other countries generally plan to award these frequencies to existing operators under DAB schemes at little or no cost, thereby not just maintaining the status quo, but expanding the reach of commercial radio firms.

As each country announces its digital radio plans, the rhetoric has generally been of increased choice coupled with improved reception. For example, the state-owned and ostensibly non-commercial

Australian Broadcasting Corporation's current fact sheet on DAB claims that: 'As Digital Radio is introduced in Australia, it's likely that listeners will get more than just a better sound from their existing AM and FM radio services. There will probably be new stations that will expand listeners' choice with specialist program formats, for example, country music, or big band swing, or sport or business, or seniors or children's radio.'[11] However, a closer look at the driving forces behind digital radio, and the plans announced so far by these commercial firms in Australia, tells quite a different story.[12]

As this book went to press, the future of DAB radio was still in play, with timetables for introduction falling behind in several countries and a growing campaign to force regulators to live up to their sales rhetoric about increased choice and community access.

Online radio

Online or internet radio is something of a misnomer, because it really isn't 'radio' at all. The similarity is in the format: shows can include DJs, music, radio documentaries, and all the usual content one associates with traditional broadcast radio.

Instead of transmitting the show over the airwaves, however, its creators upload the digital file to a web site. Listeners can then download the file for playback either in real time (live) or later on. In addition, online 'radio stations' can provide text or visual material alongside their audio files, potentially making for a rich mix of information and entertainment.

Take a trip around the world of online radio

Here are just a few web sites where you can explore innovative and original radio that's 'broadcast' via the internet:

- Radio Algérienne – music and news for Algerians around the world: www.algerian-radio.dz
- Hasda Punjab radio – Sikh and Indian community station in Canada: www.hasdapunjabradio.com
- soma fm – seven channels of San Francisco-based alternative/underground music: www.somafm.com
- Upstart Radio America – anti-war broadcasts: www.upstartradio.com
- Radio La Primerísima – community news and talk radio in Nicaragua: www.live365.com/stations/rlp680

Streaming audio technology, an innovation that allows sound to be transmitted live without annoying breaks or stops, has made online radio much more attractive for listeners and 'broadcasters' alike. Free audio software, such as RealPlayer Basic (www.real.com) and Windows Media Player (www.microsoft.com), lets computer users tune in. Additional capabilities are available with paid-for software packages. As these programmes are improved, users are gaining the ability to view DVD-quality video as well as receive streaming audio.

Sadly, the burgeoning internet radio world has recently been threatened by legislation ostensibly targeted at illegal MP3 trading sites. These laws would add extra fees for playing music online, on top of the fees online stations must already pay to music-licensing agencies like ASCAP and BMI. One online station's calculations indicated that the new fees would cost around $1,000 US per day – making online music broadcasting out of reach for non-corporate entities.[13]

Steve Dunifer: micropower and low-power alternative radio advocate

You don't have to be noisy or outgoing to make your mark in radio. Alternative radio pioneer Steve Dunifer is neither, but his work as a technical innovator and political advocate has reconfigured the micropower and low-power radio scene.

Now 53, Dunifer has been into radio since he was an 11-year-old wiring up radio circuits as a hobby. At 17, he passed his first class radio telephone licence exam, giving him the right papers to work behind the scenes as a radio and TV broadcast engineer during college. The 1960s was a radical time to be at university, and Dunifer found his attention drawn away from his studies and towards political and social activism.

Because of his interest in radio, alternative media work was always part of his political vision – his skills in this area gave him something he could contribute to causes he supported. Dunifer even considered starting his own station for a while in the late 1970s, but FCC rule changes put an end to that dream.

Since 1992, Dunifer's main project has been Free Radio Berkeley (www.freeradio.org). For five years, FRB ran an unlicensed 50-watt station in the college town of Berkeley, California. It was a 24/7 operation, with community news shows, live interviews, and an impressive range of music as well. FRB also worked to spread the tools it used for this endeavour to the wider community.

Since the FCC shut down Free Radio Berkeley as a broadcaster in 1998, spreading micropower technology has become FRB's primary

Figure 4.1 Free Radio Berkeley volunteers and would-be broadcasters at a packed microradio workshop in Haiti. (Photo: Free Radio Berkeley)

mission. FRB designs and manufactures micropower radio kits, gives out information on building and using your own equipment, and, through its IRATE (International Radio Action Training Education) arm, provides technical training for those who would operate them.

In the 1990s, Dunifer was instrumental in setting up five microradio stations in Haiti and training forty operators. FRB has also been active in Mexico, with its transmitters on air from Mexico City to Chiapas, and elsewhere.

IRATE's hands-on workshops cover basic broadcasting and electronic skills. Its popular 'Radio Camps' in Berkeley have attendees learning how to build a low-power radio transmitter and antenna – everything needed to get a station on the air – in just four days. Recently, sessions on low-power television and digital media have also been on offer.

FRB's technology work, along with the fast pace of developments in electronics in general, has been an essential element in the spread of micropower radio, Dunifer says. 'Newer and better transistors have made amplifiers much easier to design and build,' he notes, adding that 'related gear, such as audio mixers and compressor/limiters, has come down quite a lot in price over the last few years.' That's made FRB's kits work better but cost less: 'All our new amplifiers are no-tune designs, so there's no more tweaking of tuning elements,' he says. 'This makes them a lot more stable and easy to work with.'

FRB's next model will be microprocessor-controlled, with features like power monitoring and control built in. These new transmitters can be monitored and controlled over the internet or a home computer, Dunifer explains.

This has particular benefits when stations are working without a licence, because a remote, unlicensed transmitter can receive content from a legal internet streaming audio operation. 'Audio streaming allows the studio and transmitter to be separated,' Dunifer notes. 'Folks running the studio can claim to be just broadcasting over the net and not having anything do with a transmitter. Other folks can pick up the stream and feed it to a transmitter. This way only the transmitter and a cheap computer will get busted if the FCC ever decides to get a seizure order. When a warning letter shows up, the transmitter and computer can move to a new location, thereby causing a reset of the legal clock.'

Online radio tools can add extra benefits, he noted, such as allowing local community and free radio stations to receive live coverage of global events as they happen. This tactic has been used at some anti-World Trade Organisation protests, and at other events where activists want to broadcast far beyond the immediate vicinity.

Other than these applications, Dunifer thinks that online radio will have little impact on micropower broadcasting. 'In an urban area, a 50- to 100-watt free radio station can potentially reach 100,000 or more people,' he explains. 'Every listener on an internet stream takes up bandwidth, which costs money. With free radio, the only costs are the start-up ones [plus] ongoing costs such as rent, equipment upgrades, and replacement.' Of course, it's possible that the cost of internet bandwidth may come down in price to become truly competitive. But for now, broadcasting over the airwaves has some powerful financial advantages, and can also reach far more people.

'Drive-by Radio'

One of the best and easiest applications is what we call drive-by radio.

Almost every community has some sort of flea market in a public area or another type of event such as a festival. It is very easy to set up a small radio station (15 watts) on a table. Use a deep-cycle marine battery, which will power the transmitter all day. Put the antenna about 15 feet in the air with a tripod stand (weighted down with sand bags or the legs bolted to concrete blocks) and a 15-foot mast. Hang banners and hand out flyers around the area telling people to tune to the frequency you are broadcasting on. Use a portable mixer with several microphones, a CD player, and a tape player.

Encourage folks to go home and bring their mix CDs or tapes to the table for airplay. Open up the microphone for impromptu shout-outs, raps, rants, etc. It is a great way to introduce the community to radio and get their involvement – real grassroots radio.

This method works great for political actions as well, especially ongoing strike actions with picket lines and such. People drive by and wonder what is going on: banners tell them to tune to a frequency and find out. [It's] electronic leafleting ... [it's] hard to flyer cars whizzing by, but they can tune in and listen.

(Steve Dunifer, 2005)

Although mastering basic radio broadcasting technology is within reach, political factors can make micropower radio extraordinarily difficult. 'Electronically speaking, there have never been any significant issues of safety other than someone on occasion grabbing a hot soldering iron the wrong way,' Dunifer quips. 'Political hazards are probably more of an issue – the use of a transmitter in places like Burma or China will most likely get you in serious trouble, if not dead.' He added, not entirely joking, that he almost expects the FCC to 'pass jurisdiction of unlicensed radio over to Homeland Security as a terrorist activity' in the United States.[14]

Despite the roadblocks they've encountered, new low-power and micropower stations continue to pop up on a daily basis, too many for the authorities to shut down effectively. In addition, pressure from groups like Free Radio Berkeley has caused the FCC and similar regulatory agencies to consider ways of permitting licensed low-power and micropower broadcasting.

Among the first legal low-power pioneers in the US have been WSBL-LP in South Bend, Indiana, with an emphasis on minority and Spanish-language community broadcasting;[15] and KOCZ-LP in Opelousas, Louisiana, which features zydeco music, gospel, a teenager-produced health programme, and similar locally focused content.[16]

Making radio work for you

Regardless of media creators' current skill levels, radio is an accessible communications medium. The means of production for radio is undeniably inexpensive, and anyone with a working mouth and brain possesses the most important pieces of equipment.

That makes radio a potentially open field to people who may be squeezed out of other formats. For example, Carolyn Mitchell has commented that 'radio is a particularly accessible medium for women in terms of how they can learn production skills and techniques, and how they can work together to shape program schedules and tell their stories'.[17]

At Hungary's Radio C, the country's only Roma (Gypsy) station, volunteers get clued up at grassroots radio-training sessions. As a 25-year-old Roma trainee told a reporter, 'you're getting a chance, but you don't need a diploma or a special paper, only talent and interest'.[18]

The list of basic equipment needed is short. Briefly, you will need:

1. An audio source. This could be a microphone for a DJ, or a turntable, tape deck or CD player.
2. An audio mixer (available from hobby shops, such as Radio Shack, from catalogues, or online).
3. A stereo radio transmitter (available in kit form or ready-built).
4. An antenna.

Additional equipment, and specific types of kit or equipment adjustments, can improve the quality and reach of your broadcast. For detailed specifications, suggestions, and information about places that sell equipment, see the sources listed under 'Further reading' later in this chapter.

You don't even have to start your own station – although as the short list above indicates, it wouldn't be hard to do so. All you really need is to record something of interest, and convince someone to put it on the air.

Steve Dunifer sums up what drives him as a desire for 'free and open collaborative expression without government/corporate oppression and control, [broadcasting] that breaks the current stranglehold on the free expression of culture, artistic vision, news, opinions, and rants'. If that idea resonates with you, the tools and skills are easy to obtain, and the rewards, in terms both of personal satisfaction and community service, can be many.

Exercises

4.1 Making Waves and US microradio

View the film *Making Waves* (director: Michael Lahey, 2004) about the US microradio movement, available from JumpCut Films at jumpcutfilms.com/makingwaves or via the director:

Michael Lahey
Jump Cut Films
2748 Johnson Street NE
Minneapolis, MN 55418
USA

Email: mlahey22@yahoo.com
Telephone: 001 (612) 724-5202

In this film, Lahey discusses the history of microradio in the US, focusing on the activities of three very different microradio stations in Tuscon, Arizona. Discuss the film, bringing in anything you've gathered from this chapter and your readings, from media coverage of pirate radio and microradio, or from personal experience. Be sure to answer the following questions:

1. Were you surprised to see who was involved with these radio stations? Did they fit your preconception of a 'pirate radio' operator?
2. How would you classify the three stations profiled: are they alternative, activist, both, or neither?
3. What interesting uses can you think of for microradio that might be different from those shown in the film?

4.2 Radio laws and radio outlaws

Using the Internet or a telephone, find out the following information about radio broadcasting in your area. Large classes might break up into groups, with each group tackling one of these questions:

1. Is there legal status for microradio broadcasting where you live? Is there just one kind of licence, or are there different categories for different purposes?
2. If legal status is possible, how would someone go about getting a licence? What kind of special training, equipment, or financial backing, if any, is required for licence approval?
3. Regardless of legal status, approximately how many microradio stations are broadcasting in your area?

4. What are the penalties in your area for illegal broadcasting? Has anyone been prosecuted in the past decade?
5. Find out about at least one microradio station in or near your area, and tell the rest of the class about it. If you can record and play a tape or CD of a broadcast by this station, that would be ideal.

4.3 The great microradio debate

Working in two groups, prepare outside of class for a debate on micro-radio. One side should take the part of the government radio authority, the other the part of microradio activists. Your topics are:

- Government: The airwaves must be regulated.
- Activists: The airwaves should be free.

Collect material covering as many arguments for your side as possible, and prepare responses to arguments that are likely to be presented by the other side. Each team should select a spokesperson to provide an opening argument in the debate session. Once that formality is out of the way, the debate is open. An instructor can act as moderator, if needed.

Can both sides agree to a compromise position that keeps everyone satisfied?

Further reading

Cascadia Media Collective (2003) *Five Days Over Seattle: An Audio Document of Free Radio Station Y2WTKO.* CD, available from AK Press (www.akpress.org)

Clandestine Radio – web site covering unauthorised radio and TV broadcasts worldwide: www.clandestineradio.com

Community Media Association – offers advice and support for UK community radio: www.commedia.org.uk

Dunifer, S. (2003) 'Seize the airwaves! Break the corporate media's stranglehold on the free flow of information, news, artistic expression and cultural creativity', *CounterPunch,* 24 July. Online at www.counterpunch.org/dunifer07252003.html (accessed 17 November 2004).

Features on the US microradio movement: www.diymedia.net/feature/micro

Grassroots Radio Coalition: www.kgnu.org/grassroots

Jardin, X. (2004) 'Radio bicycles in Colombia stream indigenous news', *BoingBoing,* 17 September. Online at www.boingboing.net/2004/09/17/radio_bicycles_in_co.html

Media Access Project: www.mediaaccess.org

Mitchell, C. (2004) '"Dangerously feminine?": theory and praxis of women's alternative radio', in Ross, K. and Byerly, C. M., *Women and Media: International Perspectives*. London: Blackwell, pp. 157–84.

Paper Tiger TV (1992) *Low Power Empowerment: Neighbourhood Radio in Ireland and the US*. VHS videotape, available from AK Press (www.akpress.org).

Paper Tiger TV (1991) *Luis R. Beltran Tunes In to Bolivian Miners Radio*. VHS videotape, available from AK Press (www.akpress.org).

Prometheus Radio Project: www.prometheusradio.org

Radio4All: www.radio4all.org

Ruggiero, G. and Olshansky, B. (1999) *Microradio and Democracy: (Low) Power to the People*. New York: Seven Stories Press.

Sakolsky, R. and Dunifer, S. (eds) (1998) *Seizing the Airwaves: A Free Radio Handbook*. Edinburgh: AK Press.

Strauss, N. and Mandl, D. (1996) *Radiotext(e)*. New York: Semiotext(e).

5 Broadcasting beyond the corporate sphere

Most people, even those whose writing skills extend no further than a letter to the editor of their local paper, can conceive of expressing themselves in written text. The idea of using video or film is somehow more daunting – it's easy to assume that doing so would require technical skills, and budgets, far beyond your abilities.

Luckily, that's a misconception.

As with print and radio production, better skills and equipment will produce higher-quality results. But even grassroots, low-budget productions shot with a borrowed consumer-quality video camera and edited on a home computer can provide information, inspire others to action, or even simply entertain.

Basic equipment and skills

A weekend course will equip beginners with sufficient skills to operate a consumer-quality camcorder with a reasonable degree of finesse, but it's easy enough to learn the basics from continued practice with a manual close at hand. Consumer cameras are primarily point-and-shoot models. They are sufficient for many purposes, but eventually most videographers will want access to better equipment.

The main difference between home- and professional-quality cameras is that consumer equipment has few variable controls. That's great for ensuring that home movies aren't out of focus, but it can stymie any attempts to be artistic, or to use the camera in a way that the manufacturer didn't envision. Pro cameras are almost infinitely adjustable, which makes them harder to master but more versatile. They also tend to be sturdier, heavier, and considerably more expensive.

'In-between' models do exist, and probably represent the best value for money to those just starting out but serious about making video.

A microphone may be added to record high-quality sound, and you may also need lights (the cheap halogen reflector work-lights available at home repair shops will do at a pinch).

Editing – the process of putting together video segments, sound, and other elements (such as titles) to create a coherent and attractive whole – is a bit more difficult than actual filming. Computer software like iMovie and FinalCutPro puts editing within the reach of individual would-be individual producers and small groups, however.

The 'Further reading' section at the end of this chapter suggests several books that discuss equipment, how to choose it, and how to use it.

Community-access TV

In the United States, a surprising number of alternative videographers have started out in community-access television. This almost unique institution was a byproduct of wrangling over cable television licensing in the 1970s. Cable providers were required to set aside a small segment of bandwidth for 'public access', as well as for educational and government broadcasting.[1] Although the rules and facilities available differ according to the cable company involved, many public-access stations provide classes on equipment operation and production techniques to applicants. Once these classes have been completed, applicants can produce a show for broadcast and ask for airtime. Typical producers include churches, community groups, activists, and extroverts who just want to get their face on television.

For example, on the Hawaiian island of Maui, the community cable station Akaku (www.akaku.org) may offer airtime to anyone who brings in a serviceable videotape. It also encourages individuals to attend its production classes, preparing them to become certified producers. Once certified, they have free access to Akaku's facilities and equipment to produce their programmes – the only thing they'll need to pay for is videotapes or DVDs to record on.

Akaku participants produce programmes that air on five separate public-access channels carried by Oceanic Time Warner Cable. One channel is set aside for Department of Education programmes, such as TV-based classes; another channel is operated by Maui Community College. The remaining three carry a mix of government meetings, cultural programming, advice, advocacy, and just about anything else. Programmes on offer range from Hawaiian cookery to yoga to pointedly political shows like *Orwell Rolls in His Grave* and *Public Power*.

In some areas, bandwidth is set aside specifically for the use of minority populations. For instance, Channel 4 in the UK has a minority programming remit,[2] and the Indvandrer-TV station in Denmark was founded specifically to provide a broadcast outlet for ethnic minorities.

It now offers a daily variety of magazine-style, music, culture, and news programmes in languages such as Turkish and Vietnamese.[3]

Very little theoretical attention has been given to these kinds of small-scale broadcasting efforts and their role, or potential role, within communities. It has often been assumed that they are a sort of sideshow next to the 'real' media, without any influence, and of limited interest. Conflicting views have been expressed as to the effect of ethnic- and linguistic minority media in particular. While W. J. Howell has suggested that for members of linguistic minorities, hearing their language on the air gives it added 'legitimacy',[4] others have levelled criticism. For example, one study of Latina magazines in the US found that, somewhat confusedly, they pushed both assimilation and positive ethnic identity.[5]

Can similar critiques be made of broadcasting spaces used by other kinds of minority communities, such as political or cultural minorities? It's an open question.

It can certainly be said that for most of the history of television, the problems inherent in achieving 'professional' quality have unnecessarily marginalised alternative and activist projects. The advent of inexpensive digital equipment is narrowing that gulf, however, as the following section illustrates.

Undercurrents: making alternative news

In 1993, British activists found themselves under attack on multiple fronts. The new Criminal Justice Bill (CJB) specifically proposed to make direct-action protest tactics a crime. It even proposed to hit many activists' livelihood and lifestyle choices by criminalising squatting (living rent-free in abandoned buildings had made it easier to work less and campaign more) and the burgeoning rave scene. The response of several North London media activists was to found Undercurrents, a non-profit organisation designed to support grassroots direct-action campaigns.

'We were a couple of frustrated TV producers and a handful of environmental activists who began work on what would become the country's most-recognised alternative news service,' explains co-founder Paul O'Connor. 'We worked out of a cramped bedroom in North London with just a basic edit suite and a couple of borrowed camcorders.'

The group's first missive, *Undercurrents: The Alternative News Video, Issue 1*, appeared on April Fool's Day 1994, featuring the first video segment made on the CJB, just before it was signed into law officially. Videotapes were sold hand-to-hand as well as being given to mainstream press organisations, in the hope that those would pick up on the news. The following year, Undercurrents moved to Oxford in an attempt to avoid emulating the London-centric nature of the mainstream UK press. It soon launched a tactic of setting up nationally coordinated screenings of each new video – an audience of over 3,000 saw *Undercurrents 5* on its first night.

By 1997, Undercurrents had set up a protest video archive that other filmmakers and historians could draw upon. It has since launched a web presence, had its work broadcast on Channel 4, and been involved in the production of the *Video Activist Handbook* (see 'Further reading', below).

Currently, Undercurrents has branched out into teaching video activist techniques, running an annual activist film festival (BeyondTV, currently held in Swansea), and distributing grassroots news videos made by other groups. It is also involved beyond its original UK home, getting on the scene at anti-globalisation protests and doing training and collaborative work with similar organisations worldwide. It has about seven full-time workers, not all of them paid, with many others, including students at Swansea University, pitching in for specific projects or for shorter periods of time.

'Undercurrents is an alternative to a media owned by large corporations selling us products harmful to the world and its people, encouraging passive meaningless consumerism and reflecting us back at our most mundane, i.e. "reality" TV shows,' says O'Connor. 'We encourage active participation in making media, thus allowing people to understand how TV-makers manipulate our visions and understanding of the world.' The goal is not to change what the mass media does, although O'Connor notes that the constant stream of dramatic protest videos taken using camcorders has affected mainstream TV coverage of demonstrations, but to build an alternative audience, distribution network, and consensus about what's news. 'Rather than alternative, perhaps we are traditional media – aiming to build understanding and communication rather than cause conflict,' he says.

Because Undercurrents is an explicitly activist project, it places a great deal of importance on balancing up-to-the-minute content with entertainment value. 'Creativity is what we are about,' O'Connor says. 'Most people are not interested in "issues", so we encourage people to use their imagination when telling a story, but to always keep in mind the story they are trying to get across. Many "arty" videos soon end up staying on the shelf if the message isn't clear.' Undercurrents' basic advice to would-be activist filmmakers is simple: 'Always keep the audience in mind, and what actual social change you are striving for.'

As with most alternative media projects, its biggest problems are money and distribution. Although Undercurrents has been successful in attracting some foundation grants, fundraising is a constant activity. Distribution has been helped by the use of online methods, but video downloads tend to go out for free, meaning that a different method of actually paying for materials and labour must be found.

Undercurrents has come far from humble beginnings, but it hasn't been smooth sailing the whole way: thousands of pounds' worth of video equipment was smashed by the Italian police when Undercurrents caught them brutalising demonstrators in Genoa, and there have been times when continued operation was threatened by financial problems. Still, the group has continued to create video, and to encourage others to do so as well.

'To understand our motivation, turn on the news on TV and ask yourself – is this the only way to tell us about world events?', O'Connor asks. 'We figure it isn't, and have set out to prove it. And, hey, we found thousands of people are inspired by what we do! That keeps us going.'[6]

A typical day at Undercurrents
– it's not just about running around with a camcorder!

making tea	working on videos
emailing	fundraising
doing publicity	sending out videos
cleaning the office	watering plants
meeting activists	haggling for cheap deals
learning computer programs	fixing PCs
preparing and eating lunch together	sorting out screenings

How could you help a project like this now, while you're learning how to make videos?

Getting your work seen

As with other forms of alternative and activist media, the greatest challenge that non-commercial and community video- and filmmakers face is getting their creations before the public. As O'Connor noted, commercial television stations are not normally interested in their work unless it happens to trump their own news-gathering operation, as in the case of Undercurrents' Genoa G8 demonstration videos. Production quality rather than content is often the major barrier. If it looks amateurish because of shaky camerawork and poor editing, your work will simply not meet the required professional standards.

Honing your skills through continued practice and training is the only solution to this problem. Luckily, there are many avenues for obtaining help to make your productions look better. Not only do community television operations and activist video groups like Undercurrents offer training, as mentioned previously, but national and regional film councils, local colleges, community centres, and arts councils frequently have training programmes at low or no cost. For example, in the north of England video and film training is available through a regional film council, Northern Film+Media; a national media skills development programme, SkillSet; several projects aimed at ethnic minorities or youth; and many other mainstream sources. If you're really getting into it, you might even consider a university course: you'll not only have access to top technical training, but as a student you'll be able to borrow pro-quality equipment!

There are also online self-education resources for people working in film and video. These include forums where you can ask technical questions, have your scripts and ideas evaluated by peers, find out more about business practices, and keep up with industry news that may affect you. Some of these sites are semi-commercial, in that they may be attached to a production firm or carry advertising. Nevertheless, they carry no cost to you, and may provide substantial benefits. Some of the better-known sites of interest, each with its own area of emphasis, are:

- Cinema Minema: www.cinemaminima.com
- DV Republic: www.dvrepublic.com
- Exposure: www.exposure.co.uk
- The Girls Room – Notes From the Independent Underground: www.thegirlsroom.net/indie.html
- Movie-making.net: www.mwp.com
- The Movie-Marketing Blog: www.indiescene.net
- Trigger Street: www.triggerstreet.com

Distribution: the final frontier

It's not uncommon for activist media to be distributed directly to viewers, and alternative types can try it too. Some groups use web sites to give away or sell their work, others ensure that their videotapes or DVDs are made available through online and printed catalogues. Some of the better-known catalogue operations include:

- AK Press & Distribution: www.akuk.com (UK) or www.akpress.org (US). With offices in the US, England, and Scotland, AK has contacts throughout the North American and European market. Activist works are its speciality.

- Culture Shop: cultureshop.org. This distributor carries tons of activist films, including work by Undercurrents, IndyMedia, and similar producers.
- Docurama: www.docurama.com. As its name indicates, this distributor carries documentaries only.
- Last Gasp: www.lastgasp.com. Last Gasp specialises in underground comix, but carries quite a wide range of alternative and independent videos/DVDs, as well as books and magazines.
- Ventura Distribution: www.venturadistribution.com. Ventura specialises in alternative and independent film.

Some firms with catalogues, such as AK and Last Gasp, also act as bulk distributors, offering products on their lists to bookstores and other shops. There are two ways to deal with bulk distributors. In one scenario, you sell a finished product – a packaged, shrink-wrapped DVD or video – to the distributor in bulk. In the other, you license your DVD or video to a distributor, which packages it and sells it. The distributor will pay you between 40 and 60 per cent of the retail price (pre-packaged, ready-to-sell product will earn you more; although you may find that the distributor's additional margin for packaging your stuff is worth it). The distributor sells it to the retailer at a markup of around to 10 to 20 per cent, and the shop then marks it up for sale at the full price. In other words, the distributor and retailer between them pocket most of the retail price in the form of profit.

Unfortunately for media-makers, shops generally do not buy the products outright: they order a selection that they believe will sell, and are allowed to return any unsold items to the distributor. These returns will be debited from your sales.

Before contracting with a distributor, whether it's strictly a catalogue operation or one that will resell your work to retailers, ask around about its reputation. Many alternative media ventures have foundered when distributors failed to pay them on time – or ever. Ask the distributor how, and how often, it will give you an accounting of how many videos or DVDs it has shipped, and how many have been paid for or returned. Some distributors will pay you just once a year; others will pay quarterly or more often. Make sure you know, so that there will be no unwelcome surprises. It's also a good idea to work with multiple distributors, just in case one of them has problems or goes under.

You can sell directly to retailers, a system that has the added bonus of allowing you to pocket more of the retail price yourself. You may even be able to push for a 'no-returns' sale with upfront payment, if retailers are willing to take the risk on your film.

A new possibility for direct sales has recently appeared with the advent of web-based video-rental schemes. Generally speaking, major video-rental shop chains like Blockbuster have ties with major studios and high-volume business models that prevent them from carrying alternative and activist content, unless it breaks through into the mainstream, as Michael Moore's work has done. Their online competitors are able to carry more documentaries, foreign films, and offbeat titles – even online rental schemes run by video-store companies, such as Blockbuster Online (www.blockbuster.com), carry films that their retail units do not. Just a few copies sold this way will make your film available to potentially millions of renters.

One US-based company, GreenCine (www.greencine.com/main), actually specialises in independent films. A few of the major commercial players as of 2005 are listed below:

- Glowria (France): public.glowria.fr
- LoveFilm (UK): www.lovefilm.com
- Movietrak (UK): www.movietrak.co.uk
- Netflix (US): www.netflix.com
- Netleih (Germany): www.netleih.de

'Hand-selling' at conferences, concerts, or demonstrations can also work. Enterprising Third-World people have long gone door to door with videos, and there's no reason you couldn't do the same, giving or selling your product directly to friends, neighbours, and co-workers.

Public screenings

Another method of direct distribution is setting up screenings, or at least making your work available for screenings set up by others. Art-house and independent cinemas often hold film and video festivals, and have become an important outlet for alternative and activist products alike. You can contact cinemas directly, although quite a few of them are part of larger chains, such as the Europa, City Screen/Picturehouse, and Alamo networks.

One tip you can gain from successful independent distributors is that getting people to see your film isn't as easy as just getting it booked on a screen. Think about ways you can make your screening an 'event', something that attracts people who might otherwise opt for the latest Hollywood film at the metroplex. Can you provide speakers, have a contest, add a live show, or serve drinks? The US-based Alamo chain has gained a 'rabid fan base' through these kinds of techniques, with appearances by actors and directors, live sound and smell(!) effects, and comedy shows that run alongside cult movies.[7] In many ways, these 'gimmicks' hark back to the golden age of cinema, where a day at the pictures might include a singalong, a bingo game, a live show, and a couple of shorts before the feature. The reason then was competition between cinemas – now it's competition between your alternative or activist production and a myriad of other activities, from television-watching to shopping. If you want an audience that's not made up of your mother and your friends, it helps to make it something special.

Alternatively, you could bring your film to where the people already are. Screenings can also be set up in homes, clubs, churches, pubs, schools, and anywhere else where digital projection equipment is installed or can be set up. Some enterprising filmmakers have invested in their own projection kit – all you need is a portable projector, a portable DVD player, and a folding screen (even a blank wall will do at a pinch) – and taken their own work on the road.

For example, in 2004 two members of the Shooting People collective (www.shootingpeople.org) went on the road with their own portable cinema set-up, showing short British films to anyone who contacted them through their web site or text messages. For two weeks, they screened films everywhere from bookshops to college campuses.

The indie art-film network Flicker maintains a network of established alternative screening venues at www.hi-beam.net/org/showindex.html. Most of these are gallery-style arrangements with an art orientation, but some are open to other types of productions, or are different kinds of venues.

You might even consider setting up outdoor screenings. The Outdoor Cinema network in the US (www.outdoorcinema.net) provides some highly creative ideas on its web site, and the Video Activist Network (www.videoactivism.org) notes that outdoor screenings have the advantage of bringing people together in a social setting where ideas and actions are likely to be discussed.

Online video distribution

Another way to screen your work is online. Short works can be encoded as digital files and distributed through a web site. For example, DIVA TV (www.actupny.org/divatv), a New York-based AIDS activist film group, provides clips of ACT-UP actions, interviews, civil disobedience training videos, and much more on the web. Viewers can download short clips and play them back on a home computer using the free RealPlayer software package.

Even better results, and full-length films, can be obtained through broadband video links. This requires that you have a server capable of sending out a broadband transmission, and that your viewers have broadband internet access, so it can increase your costs and limit your audience. However, broadband is becoming more common, both in homes and in schools, so it's an option that quite a few alternative and activist producers are trying.

UndergroundFilm (www.undergroundfilm.org) is trying to carve out a niche as a mass distributor of digital film using the web. Its site also includes some worthwhile forums for filmmakers.

Online distribution: the copyright question

As a non-profit organisation, UndergroundFilm is also active in trying to move forward the issue of copyright protection for independent and alternative films online. Copyright (or, to be more direct, copying) is the major drawback for online distribution. Some producers, such as those working within the Independent Media Centers network (www.indymedia.org), advocate a very different approach to copyright issues. Digital video uploaded to IndyMedia sites may carry no restrictions at all on its copying and redistribution, or carry a notice restricting only commercial use, such as re-broadcast by mainstream TV networks or sale by third parties. The latter form of copyright restriction has not been tested under the existing copyright laws of most countries, and it could be difficult to pursue an offender who has made commercial use of your video. Alternatively, producers can maintain a full individual copyright, but license their work for a specific instance of online distribution – for example, to a named activist web site.

There's an active debate on how best to protect artists' commercial and moral rights in their work, while holding back the corporatisation of cultural products. Some of the places where that conversation is taking place include the free software movement, the Free Culture student organisation (freeculture.org), the non-profit group Creative Commons (creativecommons.org), the advocacy group Public Knowledge (www.publicknowledge.org) and, of course, the IndyMedia network.

Get onto the mainstream airwaves

As O'Conner mentioned in his interview, there are times when access to mainstream broadcast news or current affairs shows is in your interest, or in the interest of the mass media. If your goal is to reach as many people as possible with your message, you'll want to keep this in mind.

If you have taken footage that suddenly becomes newsworthy, it will 'sell itself' in the absence of competition. You can simply contact an appropriate news outlet directly, although you must make sure that your work has been officially protected under copyright to stave off its resale for profit. The same caveat applies if you will need to convince a station or network to take on material that you have produced, although in that case, you'll need to compete with other material on the basis of production quality and content.

Before submitting material, familiarise yourself with the conventions of the media outlet you want to target. For example, if you have produced something that might work well on a particular video-magazine show, make sure it's in the customary format, cut to the accepted length, and of a comparable quality to items that have been broadcast in the past. Stations and networks often have submission guidelines available for independent producers – make sure that you call and ask. You don't often get a second chance if your first submission was rejected because of an avoidable error.

You'll also want to give some thought to how you package your material for submission, and to the 'pitch' you send with it. It's not difficult to prepare a colourful label for a shell case, for example, preferably one with graphics that hint at the delights within. Look at what you plan to send, and ask yourself: would you bother to run the DVD you are submitting, considering the way it looks? Make sure the package includes an explanatory letter, with contact details both in the letter and on the item itself, as they may become separated later on.

Broadcast it yourself

There is another way to distribute your work, although, as with DIY radio broadcasting, legality may differ depending on where you live. Free Radio Berkeley, Steve Dunifer's group (see interview, Chapter 4), has recently come up with a workable system for television broadcasting. The video source could be a DVD player, a multi-disk DVD changer, a computer running a program made up of digital files, or a live feed. Like FRB's radio kits, these assemble-it-yourself solutions will be inexpensive ($500 to $1,100 – about £325 to £715 at the time of writing – depending on how much power you need to put behind your signal).

Systems that work on either the UHF or VHF bands have been developed, each with the ability to broadcast for four to five miles. For more information, see www.freeradio.org.

These kits should make it much easier for someone to broadcast their work, and they're not a completely new idea. During the Soviet era, pirate TV transmissions were used as a form of broadcast samizdat in Eastern Europe by groups like Poland's Solidarity. In Czechoslovakia, a remote-broadcasting set-up was 'diverted' from the state television channel to make clandestine broadcasts during the Soviet invasion of 1968. Other efforts used equipment housed in large tower blocks, intended for official broadcasts to residents, or used home-made transmitters.[8]

Many pirates still broadcast in this region, although most have long since gone legal. Similar stations thrive almost everywhere in the Third World, except for the most repressive dictatorships.[9] They are also popping up in Western Europe, particularly in Italy, where the media and the government are headed by the same man, Silvio Berlusconi. The Italian 'Telestreet' movement (www.telestreet.it) binds together almost 200 micro-broadcasters, who often utilise common equipment originally designed for receiving broadcasts, not for transmission. In *Telestreet*, a short film by Andrew Lowenthal, Italian media critic Franco Berardi describes it as 'a technical project, a political project, [and] a cultural project'.[9]

Independent documentary-making: an interview with Michael Dean

In the past few years, there's been a resurgence in the popularity of documentary filmmaking, with projects like Morgan Spurlock's *Super Size Me*, Errol Morris's *The Fog of War*, and Michael Moore's *Fahrenheit 9/11* getting the kind of attention, distribution, and income that usually only attend feature films. This has opened the door for young filmmakers who want to tackle serious subjects, and who work outside the studio system (almost all documentary production is done by independents, although particularly successful documentary-makers may now gain some funding from major studios, as well as distribution deals).

Michael Dean used to be a singer in a rock band; now he's a filmmaker. He didn't pack in music for film school, he just picked up a camera and began using it. 'I always wanted to make films, but it was too expensive until the advent of DV technology,' he explains, 'then I grabbed it, early, and ran with it. Self-taught.'

His first major project was a film that tries to inspire others to do the same: *DIY or DIE: How to Survive as an Independent Artist*, released in 2004. He has also produced a well-received book that lays out the nuts and bolts of making movies on a shoestring, the aptly named *$30 Film School*.

'I've usually done my art indie-stylie because no one was inviting me to join the big boys,' he says, although he follows that statement by admitting that 'one of the least satisfying experiences I've ever had in three decades of making art was the 18 months my band was on a major label'.

How should you get started? Don't wait for someone else to tell you that, Dean says. Get some basic equipment, start working with it, and see where it takes you. Here's his list of your minimum do-it-yourself film-making kit:

- Camera: any three-chip DV camera. If you can't afford it, get a used Sony DCR-PC100 (a one-chip camera that has an image that looks better than some three-chip cameras).
- Microphone: Audio Technica, Model ATR-35S Omnidirectional Lavaliere Microphone. There's tons of them new on eBay for like 30 bucks.
- Any fast computer, Mac or PC (though you'll get more bang for your buck with a PC).
- A good editing program. For PC, I'd use Avid Express. For Mac, Final Cut. Or if you're just starting out, a student version of Premiere, for Mac or PC.

Dean's current project is a documentary on the controversial American writer Hubert Selby Jr, author of *Last Exit to Brooklyn*, *Requiem for a Dream*, and other novels. 'I'm making my new film, *Hubert Selby, Jr. It'll be Better Tomorrow*, on my own terms,' Dean says. 'We already have a tacit promise of representation from a large distributor, based on an 18-minute rough cut we showed them three months ago. We're currently polishing the full cut (about 100 minutes) and haven't even bothered to send them another copy. We're not showing it to anyone outside of Selby's family and a few filmmakers and screenwriters who are *in* the film, whose opinions we trust. We know the film we want to make, and don't need outside input.'

'When we're completely done, we'll take it to the mountain and lay it before the feet of the profit prophets, who will bring it from my bedroom to the world.'

Dean maintains that independent production actually allows film-makers more freedom than big budgets do, because they can maintain control over the end product. It's not just for small, one-person efforts either – for *Hubert Selby, Jr. It'll be Better Tomorrow*, Dean has worked closely with an editor and co-producer, Ryan Brown, and quite a bit of the interview footage being used has been taken by others. 'I think you can scale DIY techniques to bigger projects – I don't feel that being a self-starter includes a declaration of poverty,' he says. 'I just think it points you *away* from excess, and [away] from being co-opted or diluted.'

He points to another Selby-related project as an example: Darren Aronofsky's film adaptation of *Requiem for a Dream*. 'He did that for $4 million, on his own terms, on his own "movie lot" in Brooklyn – a warehouse he rented and built all the sets in,' Dean explains. 'A Hollywood studio would have spent $30 million making that film and it wouldn't have looked as cool. Actually, a Hollywood studio would never have made that movie … several turned it down. Darren made the film *he* wanted and then sold it to Hollywood. That's the way to do things. Major media conglomerates don't know anything about art. They only know how to sell things. They've raised *marketing* to an art. Just make your own thing, and only involve the suits when it's time to take it to the marketplace.'

Dean has a few more tips for nascent filmmakers, especially those with an activist bent:

- **Choose a subject people want to know about**: 'Michael Moore picks great subjects. He makes films that *need* to be made, films that the world wants to see. That's key.'
- **Make your project entertaining**: 'If it's boring, I don't care how important it is, I ain't gonna watch it. Dude, I would rather watch the cheeziest VH1 *Behind the Music* special about some has-been hair metal band than something that's important but boring. You have to remember that today you are dealing with an audience who grew up watching MTV and media products influenced by MTV and by advertising. I'm not saying your stuff has to have 50 cuts per minute, but at least tell a *story*.'
- **Consider alternative modes of distribution**: 'Check out the film *Outfoxed* (www.outfoxed.org). It's a very well-done media-activist flick with a very good message and it's getting a lot of attention. One thing they're doing is selling copies really cheap. On my film *DIY or DIE*, I encouraged people to make personal copies. I would have sued anyone who pressed up a few thousand and sold them, but I love it when someone makes five copies and gives them to their band or their roommates. Check out the Lost Film Fest (www.lostfilmfest.com) – they have it *down*. They are the experts in getting anarchist, leftist material out there to the *people*. They make cheap DVDs. They take stuff on tour.' When the message is more important than the money, he adds, do whatever will get your message out there.
- **Be ready to work incredibly hard, for incredibly long hours**: 'I will always make my art my own damn way, even if the budgets down the

line end up with a few extra zeros at the end,' Dean concludes. 'I'm so used to making good stuff for *nothing*, I know that I could really make stellar art for *something*.'[11]

Exercises

5.1 Dissecting the evening news

For this exercise, you'll need to tape one night's full primary newscast, from either a regional or a national station. The goal is to reduce it to its component parts, and then see what is indicated by what you find.

Working together (it may be easiest to divide the tasks up), take it apart to answer the following questions:

1. What are the running order and the length of the segments?
2. What is each news segment about?
3. Who narrates each segment?
4. Which people have been chosen for interviews? List their names and titles/occupations if provided, and classify them by class, gender, race, etc.
5. Who seems to have the most authoritative voice in each segment? Is it the presenter, one of the interviewees, or perhaps even a subject who is being covered?
6. What visuals are used in each segment?
7. Is any seemingly objective data presented, such as percentages, graphs, charts, or attributions to research? What is the source of this information, if known?
8. Are any metaphors used in the text, visuals or both?

Now, taking this descriptive data and your own impressions of the broadcast, discuss the following as regards each segment, and the broadcast as a whole:

1. What issues or events have been given the most airtime?
2. Can you make any deduction about who these issues or events would affect most?
3. Are the events or issues reported on put into context, or reported as isolated incidents?
4. Do the visuals used support or subtly change the message being given verbally?
5. Who is most likely to be presented to viewers as an authority?
6. How about the language used? Do the metaphors used, if any, or the way people or events described, tell you how the news broadcasters want you to interpret their reports?

7. Do any segments seem designed to move viewers to act on the information provided in any way? If so, how?

Your analysis may be informed by books from the 'Further reading' list for this chapter, below, particularly those by Iyengar and Clemencia Rodríguez. The FrameWorks Institute also provides some worthwhile guidance on its own recommended method on its web site at www.frameworksinstitute.org/strategicanalysis/perspective.shtml.

5.2 Distributing your own 'evening news'

Starting with the lessons taken from Exercise 5.1, or from the Undercurrents interview earlier in this chapter, come up with a clever plan for getting a locally made, video-based broadcast news show to people in your town. Make sure you avoid typical pitfalls, such as preaching to the converted (or its student counterpart, talking only to other students). What factors are likely to make people want to see your show? Which of the many methods of distribution discussed in this chapter might work for you, and why? Can you think of others? How can you inform people about the broadcast, or get the video/DVD into their hands?

5.3 ViVe Television: a new model for community broadcasting?

In Venezuela, the government has recently launched several initiatives charged with making more democratic media available, and for getting independently produced, local content onto national TV and radio. One of these initiatives, ViVe Television, is an experiment in mixing a strong proportion of local and national productions with those from elsewhere in Latin America, in an effort to combat the influence of the North American content that pervades most other Venezuelan TV. Find out about the background of ViVe Television and the people who run it, what programming it presents, and how it has been received. Share this information in the form of a paper, an oral presentation, or in a multimedia format.

Here are two sources to help you get started:

- ViVe Television: www.vive.gov.ve
- Podur, J. (2004) 'Venezuelan community TV: an interview with Blanca Eekhout, director of ViVe', *Z Magazine*, 6 September 2004. Online at www.zmag.org/content/showarticle.cfm?SectionID=45& ItemID=6174

Further readings

Baumgarten, P., Farber, D. C., and Fleischer, M. (1992) *Producing, Financing and Distributing Film: A Comprehensive Legal and Business Guide.* Pompton Plains, NJ: Limelight Editions.

Boyle, D. (1997) *Subject to Change: Guerrilla Television Revisited.* Oxford: Oxford University Press.

Dean, Michael W. (2003) *$30 Film School.* New York: Muska & Lipman/Premier-Trade.

DIY Convention/DIY Film Festival: www.diyconvention.com

Goldberg, K. (1990) *The Barefoot Channel: Community Television as a Tool for Social Change.* Vancouver, BC: New Star.

Goodell, G. (1998) *Independent Feature Film Production: A Complete Guide From Concept Through Distribution.* New York: St Martin's Griffin.

Halleck, D. (2002) *Hand-Held Visions: The Possibilities of Community Media.* Bronx, NY: Fordham University Press.

Harding, T. (2001) *The Video Activist Handbook.* London: Pluto Press.

Iyengar, S. (1991) *Is Anyone Responsible? How Television Frames Political Issues.* Chicago: University of Chicago Press.

Newton, D. and Gaspard, J. (2001) *Digital Filmmaking 101: An Essential Guide to Producing Low-Budget Movies.* Studio City, CA: Michael Weise Productions.

Rodríguez, C. (2001) *Fissures in the Mediascape: An International Study of Citizens' Media.* Cresskill, NJ: Hampton Press.

Rodríguez, R. (1996) *Rebel Without a Crew.* New York: Plume Books.

Ryan, C. (1991) *Prime-Time Activism: Media Strategies for Grass-Roots Organizing.* Boston: South End Press.

Salzman, J. (2003) *Making the News: A Guide for Activists and Nonprofits.* Boulder, CO: Westview Press.

Wayne, M. (1998) *Dissident Voices: The Politics of Television and Cultural Change.* London: Pluto Press.

6 Artistic impulses

Some forms of alternative media act primarily or secondarily as venues for explorations in design, the artistic process, or the exercise of creativity for its own sake. Well-known examples include the *San Francisco Oracle* newspaper, which was a prime example of the 'hippie' aesthetic in 1960s underground publishing; the pioneering 1980s digital design magazine *Émigré*, which championed computer-based design work in print long before mainstream graphic artists and advertising companies picked up on it; and Artists' Television Access, a San Francisco-based organisation that has been encouraging experimental videography since 1984.

This chapter examines ways that alternative artistic visions have been presented in a variety of alternative (and sometimes activist) media, including the three examples just mentioned.

Experiments, influences, and moments in time

For a paper that lasted for just two years (1966–8) and twelve issues, the *San Francisco Oracle* has retained its aura for a very long time. It was a worker-owned cooperative, started with donations from a friendly Haight Street shopkeeper and his brother. Much of the manual labour for production and distribution was provided by its contributing artists and writers. What made it an artistic endeavour was its celebration of psychedelic imagery, long before it had become a staple of 'hip' clothing and record advertisements.

New, and expensive, printing techniques were tried to made the paper's colourful covers and centrefolds sparkle. The use of special screens, overlays, and unique inks made the rainbow-hued paper a 'psychedelic experience' in itself, even before the addition of experimental poetry and calls to enhanced consciousness or political action. 'To achieve the oracular effects we wanted we would give the text, whether prose or poetry, to artists and ask them to design a page for it, not merely to illustrate it, but to make an organic unity of the word and the image,' *Oracle* co-founder the late Allen Cohen once said.[1]

The *Oracle* is archived at the University of California at Davis (www.oac.cdlib.org/findaid/ark:/13030/kt1x0nc2p3), and bound facsimile editions are available. Although it's still worth looking at, its swirling, psychedelic style doesn't now have the shock of the new that it delivered in its day.

But in every generation there are designers who push the envelope. In the 1980s, the action was in the new field of digital typography and design. New typefaces by imaginative designers like Neville Brody, best known for his contributions to the cutting-edge independent music magazine *The Face*, made it possible to create and play with design ideas old and new.

Émigré, a Bay Area design magazine associated with its own digital type 'foundry', was another notable site for experimentation. You can see a collection of its groundbreaking cover designs at www.emigre.com. You will immediately notice that these ideas are still influencing print design in the twenty-first century. *Émigré*'s innovations included mixing typefaces, twisting type into shapes, and the use of type as a pure design element. In this magazine, the design was the message – but then again, its intended audience was designers.

One issue of *Émigré* focused on a quite different design trend, a highly personalised, high-touch, handmade style associated mostly but not exclusively with independent music. Bruce Licher's Independent Project Press and Records, for example, made limited-edition album covers, packaging designs, handbills, and even concert tickets. These media artefacts were seen as collectable art objects as well as functional items created to draw attention to bands like Savage Republic.

Licher used antique presses, and frequently printed on unusual materials, such as chipboard and cardboard. As Licher told one interviewer, 'I had already made a couple of records and I was interested in creating an art record – one that would be packaged in a way that would have the feel of a limited-edition art project.'[2]

A few examples of Licher's print design work, including some Independent Project Press and Records designs, can be seen online at www.mobilization.com and www.creativerefuge.com/pages/spotlight. htm.

The dichotomy of computer-based, slick design and 'high-touch' individualised design is one that nourishes today's designers. It breaks down the artificial barriers between 'fine arts' and media, resulting in artwork that takes the form of books, zines, magazines, posters, recordings, and films.

Media projects like the *Oracle*, *Émigré*, and Independent Project Press and Records can be said to have captured and even created the artistic feel of a specific time and place, reflecting the interests of emerging subcultures and technologies. Although they had a limited lifespan, their influence continues – at least in part because their vision was captured in media products that were reproduced and disseminated well beyond the confines of galleries or museums.

Making media arts

Other art-focused alternative and activist media projects aim to provide venues for a multitude of styles, formats, and points of view. For example, Artists' Television Access (www.atasite.org), based in a shopfront in the Mission district of San Francisco, has both introduced artists to media production, and encouraged would-be videographers to think of themselves as artists. It has also played an important part in getting local activists into documentary production.

ATA started life as a traditional art gallery, but so many of the artists exhibiting in the 1980s were doing hybrid work that incorporated video or film that it transmogrified into something almost unique for that era: a full-service resource centre for helping artists make video, and videographers make art. It has made a point over the years of involving San Francisco's gay, lesbian, and transgender community; holds both mixed and women-only technical classes; and has been instrumental in training an entire generation of Black, Asian, and Hispanic video artists.

For most visitors, ATA's first attraction is the excellent equipment on offer. If you've already shot some film but don't have the luxury of your own editing suite, ATA can provide the space and equipment to turn it into a final product. If you need somewhere to show your finished video, ATA turns into a video- and film-gallery space most evenings. A wide variety of low-cost technical classes is available. Hang around for a while, however, and you'll find that the most important resource at ATA is the people who use it. Creative cross-fertilisation has led to 'conceptual art' going out live on pirate radio, hip-hop musicians who came in to make music videos ending up writing scores for activist films, and activists thinking beyond 'talking heads' to create innovative and entertaining documentaries.

ATA is run by a group of about thirty volunteers and a very few paid part-timers. Funding comes from donations, grants, small equipment-rental fees, and low admission charges for screenings.[3]

Similar centres have since opened up in many other cities and a few rural areas as well, each configured to meet the needs of the community in which it's situated. A few examples are: the World Beat Center (www.worldbeatcenter.org), serving San Diego's African-American community; Seattle's 911 Media Arts Center (www.911media.org); and the Media Arts Project in Asheville, North Carolina (www.themap.org).

Like ATA, these organisations provide the space, equipment, and expertise to help others realise their artistic vision in media formats. It's also possible to fulfil many of these requirements without establishing a permanent physical base. For example, the Flicker site (www. hi-beam.net/cgi-bin/flicker.pl) provides ongoing virtual screenings of art films in digital formats online, and also hosts announcements, contacts listings, and a discussion list.

Putting art inside the media

Still other projects seek to change existing media formats by making them more accessible to artists, or by bringing in an artistic, experimental sensibility.

Billing itself as 'London's first art radio station', Resonance FM radio (www.resonancefm.com) is a prime example of this kind of venture. Run by the London Musicians Collective (www.l-m-c.org.uk), its broadcasts are, to say the least, eclectic and unique. A single day might roam from a half-hour show featuring the sounds of unusual instruments to free-styling DJs mixing up music and noise.

Resonance FM 'differs precisely in its approach to the medium: Resonance views radio as raw material to be used for aesthetic purposes, rather than defining the medium primarily in terms of its civic role (public radio) or money-making potential (commercial radio)', explains co-founder Ed Baxter. 'At every level it is a project distinct from either of the other tiers in British broadcasting.'

The station actually began as a print magazine about the arts, *Resonance*, which published an inspirational issue on radio arts. This spawned a short-term, one-month arts broadcasting project under the terms of a restricted service licence. When the UK government decided to make low-power radio licences available to organisations under the Pilot Access scheme in 2001, the group behind this broadcast applied and was successful.

As always, the greatest impediment to this alternative media format has been money, Baxter says. Pilot Access licensing terms were for twelve months at a time, so attracting well-heeled sponsors and a sizeable core of listeners was difficult. 'We took out an overdraft and for about a year it was touch and go on a monthly basis as to whether we could continue,' he admits. 'All the while we tried to prove our worth and our good business sense.' So far, Resonance FM has survived thanks to the dedication of volunteers and the occasional grant or fundraising event.

Now that the station is on a slightly more even keel financially, it's been able to do more art and less business. It's been surprisingly difficult to get listeners and radio practitioners to let go of their own preconceptions about 'proper' radio practices and formats, allowing new ideas to get on the air. 'In Britain, people have a very rigid view of what constitutes radio,' Baxter explains. 'For instance, they think it is a legal requirement to have weather and news broadcasts. For the first year or so, we regularly got emails asking if Resonance was a joke.'

The rapid spread of accessible, low-cost audio technology has played an important part in the station's success, he added: 'Nowadays editing, montage, and recording technology is readily available, and one can make a programme on a laptop in a single day.' The availability of these tools has opened up possibilities, because the best way to extend and change an existing medium is, as Baxter says, 'by doing it'. The process is the art form just as much as the end product is, he says, requiring 'pragmatic decisions, experimentation, not knowing what you can do or can get away with – that is how any form develops. Imagination and above all (in this case) the context where experimentation makes sense are important: without the support structure that Resonance offers, stretching the form and content would make no sense.'[4]

Art as alternative media

In a fascinating article called 'Accidents should happen: cultural disruption through alternative media',[5] Daniel Makagon makes a strong case for certain forms of public art practices as alternative and activist media. He links these back to Surrealist and Situationist projects that blended art practices and political motives, particularly those aimed at getting people to see the urban environment in new and subversive ways. For example, graffiti, such as the well-known Situationist slogan painted on Paris walls in 1968 – 'beneath the paving stones, the beach!' – can invite the viewer to consider how the built environment shapes his or her movements and desires. Performance art projects that confound one's expectation of what will happen in public places also fit this description. They are media because their reason for being is the communication of ideas, but they are media of a very specific type.

Makagon concentrates on two artists, Jenny Holzer and Krzysztof Wodiczko, who create this kind of public art-as-communication. For instance, Holzer has placed challenging and unexpected messages on the marquees of Times Square theatres and on street posters. Wodiczko's projects include images projected onto buildings, drawing attention to the messages already 'written' into the public environment through building design, urban planning, and the prescribed uses of space.

Other forms of media – print, radio, video, etc. – can be so familiar that the messages they carry are lost in the well-worn formulas of formatting and consumption practices. When these media are used in different ways, the result may be viewed as 'art' rather than as media products per se. That act of stepping outside of conventional forms can set up a different dialogue between media creators and media consumers.

As Makagon writes of Wodiczko's work: 'outside the confines of a theater – with its requisite call for silence – public projection allows for conversation and debate ... projections ultimately offer us an opportunity to explore new conceptions and diverse uses of media technologies.'[5] Art practices that take media forms out of their expected context may provoke public discussions, and raise questions that would seem leaden in the verbose prose of a scholarly article on urban design.

Case study: 'Life: a user's manual'

Canadian media performance artist Michelle Teran uses dramatic techniques, including costumes and props, and media technology to raise questions about surveillance and security in the modern city.

Dressed as a homeless person, she pushes a shopping trolley through the streets of major cities like Utrecht and Brussels. The trolley is piled high with TV sets – but these aren't the urban discards one might expect. Teran also carries an antenna and video scanner tuned to capture images from the hundreds of CCTV cameras she passes along the way. These images are rebroadcast in her cart.

As Teran writes: 'Both public physical spaces and private interior spaces contain traces of fragmentary personal [hi]stories tied together by an invisible network of media.'[7] Her work seeks to reveal ways that this network functions.

This performance raises multiple questions in a highly visual and interesting way. For example, it's often said that good neighbours 'look out for each other'. In most urban neighbourhoods, it is CCTV cameras and the remote staff who monitor them that do most of the 'looking'. When they capture the image of a homeless woman, the focus may be on her criminality (vagrancy and rough sleeping are, technically, crimes in almost all cities) or her 'otherness'. How might this gaze differ from that of a resident who sees the homeless woman on the block as part of his or her neighbourhood? What actions and reactions may result from these two different acts of looking?

This kind of art isn't decorative or entertaining. It challenges ideas and activities, in the same way as a newspaper editorial or TV documentary might. Because it uses media forms in a unique way, however, it allows witnesses to step out of their preconceived notions for a few minutes. Some may find themselves thinking about whose security our pervasive surveillance system actually supports. A few may come to conclusions that lead to social or political action.

You can follow one of Teran's walks, preserved through electronic media, at www.impaktonline.nl/box/life.

Art as activism

The activist message in works like Michelle Teran's is implicit, not explicit. You could find her work fascinating simply because it reveals a hidden world of media images on our city streets, or admire its aesthetic qualities and playfulness. Other media art practices may be explicitly activist, conceived and executed with the express purpose of provoking a political reaction or making a political point.

Many such actions can be traced back to the 'guerrilla theatre' movement of the 1960s, which was made up of both formal theatre groups, like the San Francisco Mime Troupe (www.sfmt.org) and looser adherents, like the Diggers (www.diggers.org) and Yippies (members.aol.com/stewa/stew.html). The Mime Troupe used the forms of *commedia dell'arte*, a style of theatre employing much slapstick and farce that dated back to Renaissance Europe. The Diggers, Yippies, and similar groups were proponents of socio-political pranksterism, amongst other activities. For example, when middle-class tourists came to the Haight-Ashbury district in San Francisco to stare at the hippies, some Diggers held up mirrors to the windows of their tour buses, inviting sightseers to view *themselves* as objects of amusement and derision instead.

Some 'guerrilla theatre' pranks were more in the line of theatrical media events, designed to attract the attention of jaded reporters by providing the sort of colourful, entertaining spectacle that is certain to command a spot on the evening news. Although participants have claimed that they didn't inform the press in advance about their actions, when a group of Yippies threw money into the broker's pit at the New York Stock Exchange, the story was instantly picked up by the newspapers.

Indeed, since many media outlets see marches and traditional protests as passé and/or unworthy of reportage, activists since the 1970s have increasingly looked for ways to make a splash through creative, eye-catching actions. Steve Durland examined this phenomenon by classing the media-savvy protest work of the environmental group Greenpeace as a form of performance art. He quotes Greenpeace activist Steve Loper, who helped hang a banner from the Statue of Liberty that said 'Give Me Liberty From Nuclear Weapons, Stop Testing', as saying: 'Every August 6th [the anniversary of the Hiroshima atomic bomb] the media is looking for an image that denotes protests against nuclear weapons. What we did in '84 was give them the perfect image. It was one of the most enjoyable [actions] I've done.' Greenpeace could have issued a press release, produced a pamphlet, or held a march to mark the occasion, but a dramatic action that resulted in a bold media image was deemed more likely to get its message across. Durland calls such actions 'effective creativity with a mission'.[8]

Activist groups planning public events now worry about looking boring, and often choose to concoct outrageous spectacles. 'Protest performance' groups like the Radical Cheerleaders (radcheers. tripod.com/RC) and the Billionaires for Bush (billionairesforbush.com) contingent, whose irony-drenched appearances so enlivened the 2004 US presidential campaign, are seen to add vitality and much-needed colour to demonstrations. Many also believe that attention-getting actions can get a message across better than earnestly passing out leaflets or taking part in repetitive chants. As *The Activist Cookbook: Creative Actions for a Fair Economy* puts it, in a discussion of some theatrical actions executed by anti-poverty group United for a Fair Economy, 'If the housing jester hadn't changed costume on his way to the supermarket, sure, people would have taken the leaflets but they wouldn't have been charmed or intrigued. If the film activists had held a private protest screening or the tour organizers had held a standard rally, there would have been no direct dramatic challenge to the target, no media spectacle, and consequently a lot less pressure.'[9]

Critical Art Ensemble (www.critical-art.net), an art and theory collective that has been very active in this area of work, classifies much of it as 'tactical media', media actions that are part of an organised political campaign, rather than art per se. Although it's nothing new (some might simply call it propaganda, although much does not fit the classical definition of that term), tactical media is definitely an area where a great deal of creativity is fermenting.

Incidentally, in 2004 two members of the Critical Art Ensemble were charged with violations of the USA PATRIOT Act for an art project about germ warfare that involved the use of scientific apparatus and harmless bacteria (see www.caedefensefund.org for more details). For some observers, at least, activist media arts can be perceived as a real threat, not just an effete art project. (Tactical media is covered in greater detail in Chapter 10.)

Art as activism can take place in the streets or in a gallery – it all depends on how the project is conceived and carried out, and who the intended audience is. Some artists create mobile projects that may move through many different environments: Michelle Teran's 'Life: a user's manual' project, described earlier in this chapter, exemplifies this genre. Others create art events in public places, often seeking to involve members of the public as active participants (the Living Theatre's 'Code Orange Cantata' is one such project: see www.livingtheatre.org for more information). Others, like Critical Art Ensemble, use artistic techniques to illuminate political theory or to educate.

Exercises

6.1 DIY or DIE: Screening and discussion

For this exercise, you'll need a copy of Michael Dean's film, *DIY or DIE*, discussed in the interview with Dean in Chapter 5. View the film, and discuss the following:

1. Each of the people interviewed in this film has found a way to 'live for art'. Citing examples from the interviews, how might that differ from 'making a living from art'?
2. In the interview with Ian MacKaye, he is very articulate about his belief that commercialising art in a corporate way changes what it's all about. Can you relate this to the definitions of alternative media discussed in Chapter 1?
3. This film was made by one person, and cost just under $10,000 (about £6,500). As an example of alternative media itself, how well does it work for you? Would it have got its message across more effectively with slicker production values, or other changes? What would you have done differently?

6.2 Art and activism: where's the border?

Present a case, using evidence, background research, and examples, for one of the following positions:

1. When art is used to push a political point of view, the result is nothing more than propaganda.
2. Artistic work can enrich political actions and debate, but it can also distract from putting across a clear political message.
3. All art is political, just as every human action is political. Therefore, you cannot divide art from activism.

Further reading

Adbusters magazine: adbusters.org/home

Art-icles – international media arts news magazine: videopool.typepad.com/articles_international_me

Billboard Liberation Front and Friends (1996) *The Art and Science of Billboard Improvement.* Tucson, AZ: See Sharp Press.

Critical Art Ensemble (2001) *Digital Resistance: Explorations in Tactical Media.* New York: Autonomedia.

Critical Art Media (1996) *Electronic Civil Disobedience and Other Unpopular Ideas.* New York: Autonomedia.

Dana, R. (1986) *Against the Grain: Interviews with Maverick American Publishers.* Iowa City, IA: University of Iowa Press.

Fusco, M. and Hunt, I. (2004) *Put About: A Critical Anthology of Independent Publishing.* London: BookWorks.

National Alliance for Media Arts and Culture (NAMAC): www.namac.org

Ruby, K. (2000) *Wise Fool Basics: A Handbook of Our Core Techniques.* Berkeley, CA: Wise Fool Puppet Interventions.

Thompson, N. and Sholette, G. (eds) (2004) *The Interventionists: Users' Manual for the Creative Disruption of Everyday Life.* Cambridge, MA: MIT Press.

United for a Fair Economy (1997) *The Activist Cookbook: Creative Actions for a Fair Economy.* Boston, MA: United for a Fair Economy.

Wakefield, S. and Grrrt (2003) *Not for Rent: Conversations With Creative Activists in the UK.* Second edition. New York: Evil Twin Publications.

7 Creating media spaces for the personal

Not all forms of alternative media are group-oriented. This chapter looks at 'zines' and small publishing ventures by individuals that bring intensely personal views to a wider audience.

It begins with a story, written in response to a short, simple question: 'Why publish?'

When I was in the first grade I entered the world of self-publishing with a hand-printed and illustrated booklet on the neighborhood mutts called *The Inbred Crossbred Dog Book*. Round about the age of eight my father gave me my very own 'home printing press' (actually, a gelatin printing set – a tray, gelatin mix, special inked paper. You type on the paper, set it on the gelatin, which picks up an inverted picture, then lay clean paper on to the now-inked gelatin to make a printed page). I made my own newspaper called, I think, *The Neighborhood News*. Sample item:

> 'A poem'
>
> White beans and cornbread
> They have them at school
> Then we have them at home I hate
> White beans and cornbread

Such is life to a four-eyed clumsy kid growing up in her cousin's oversized hand-me-downs in Paducah, Kentucky, OK? In junior high I wrote bad poetry and worse romantic socialist political manifestos (in my diary, thank goodness, so none of my more-anarcho-than-thou friends will ever see them). In high school I did a one-shot underground newspaper, *The Tilghman Hell* (lovingly named after the official school paper, *The Tilghman Bell*, and printed

---

by the folks at *The Subversive Scholastic* up in Columbus, Ohio – are they still around, by the way?).

Somewhere in there I discovered punk rock and – is this all fitting together? – ended up taking pictures of rad 'fridge dives for *Mutual Oblivion* zine in Albuquerque, then doing *Drool Beat* back in my hometown and, for the past couple of years, bringing out *Incoherent House* – now called *Incoherent*.

Anyway, so much for the history.

The answer is: what else could I possibly do with my time? How better could I waste my munificent welfare checks? How else could I get up the courage to talk to people at shows? 'Wanta buy a zine?' isn't much as opening lines go, but it's the best this congenitally shy gal can do.[1]

That's a picture of this book's author, twenty-odd years ago.

For at least some of us, publishing is something that's bred in the bone. We feel compelled to do it for many different reasons. In Mike Gunderloy's compilation of zine-makers' stories, *Why Publish?*, reasons given range from loneliness and boredom to a desire to change the world, one reader at a time.

'I don't care about convincing people, I care about meeting people who have a vision similar to mine,' one zinester wrote; 'I wanted to become part of the local underground music scene [but] have no talent musically,' said a second; 'writing and publishing is a hobby with me, like music, flying, and baking cookies', wrote a third.[2]

One very important reason is that there is little room for personal vision in the mainstream media. Opinion and 'slice-of-life' columns exist in abundance, but are usually commissioned to get a prestigious 'name' writer on board, or to fill a niche by appealing to a specific target audience, such as new parents or Asian readers. When this kind of writing serves a commercial purpose, it is pursued; when it does not, it's edited away or dropped altogether. Even writers who have access to space in commercial newspapers and magazines sometimes feel the itch to express themselves without the filter of editing, and without having to worry about whether what they write will appeal to advertisers or the general public. Personal media can fill that need, among others.

Private, personal, and beyond

Personal media products can be produced on a scale that ranges from tiny to, potentially, reaching over 100,000 readers. At the smallest end of

Figure 7.1 Fanzine formats and content can differ wildly. From left to right, a personal zine, *Incoherent House*; semi-glossy indie music zine *Puncture*; a typical cut-and-paste punk zine, *Drool Beat*; and *Guinea Pig Zero*, a work-zine for medical experiment subjects. (Photo: Mitzi Waltz)

the concept is private publishing: creating media for a specific and small number of individuals who are known to you. Such media could be hand-made, even hand-delivered, and financial considerations would not enter into the picture. The exercises at the end of this chapter will encourage you to give this kind of small-scale project a try. The experience may whet your appetite for more.

The next level up is small-scale personal publishing, where the media product's creators actively try to distribute it to people who they hope will find it interesting. In his book *Alternative Media*, Chris Atton argues that 'the lived relationship of the individual zine writer to the world, from which position develops the possibility of the social',[3] is the guiding principle for this kind of project. He points to self-valorisation as a key function for zine writers.

It can be argued that zine readers also seek self-valorisation through their consumption of zines that mirror their own views, that make them feel as if they are part of a social group (albeit one whose members may never meet in person), or even that challenge their views and identities in ways that help them clarify their beliefs.

At its greatest level of volume, the zine world in the 1980s and 1990s was actually a highly social system of its own, with a system of zine-for-zine barter that encouraged communication, and publications (such as Mike Gunderloy's *Factsheet Five* magazine) that existed solely to inform people about zines. A network of personal contacts formed between zine writers, editors, and readers that often spilled off the printed page and into 'real life': friendships, romances, feuds, apartment shares, travel plans, bands, and organisations formed that began with one person picking up another person's zine. The larger zine community was relatively diverse, as zines might cover anything from science fiction to punk rock to paganism. Within that totality, there were sub-groups, but cross-topic communication was not uncommon. As Atton says, zines present 'an individual's declaration and construction of self-identity and [invite] others to engage in a dialogue about that identity'.[4]

Java Turtle: a personal zine story

In 1996, Lynne Lowe was shopping for clothes when she came across her first fanzine. She had no idea that there were thousands of these small, self-published magazines around until, completely by coincidence, she came across a copy of *Factsheet Five* later that same week. 'I was shocked to discover that it was full of zines and alternative comics that I could send for,' she says. 'For the next few weeks I sent for many titles and made daily runs to my post office box. I spent many wonderful hours reading in my favorite coffeehouse.' Within six months, she had started work on a zine of her own.

Her biggest inspiration was *Murder Can Be Fun*: editor John Marr 'writes amazing true life stories about murders, kidnappings, disasters and other delights of craziness and mayhem,' Lowe says. 'You could tell how much research he put into each issue.' But there were dozens of others that piqued her interest, from the daily-life chronicles of *Cometbus* and *Dishwasher* to highly political titles like the *Match*.

Ideas for *Java Turtle* came from her personal experiences and interests, and most issues were organised around a theme. 'Some issues are no-brainers: I get an idea and go with it,' Lowe says. For one issue, she asked several artist friends to draw a story or a picture about coffee (as the zine's name indicates, Lowe is a self-declared 'java junkie'). 'I got so many submissions that I couldn't publish all of them,' she says. 'That issue sold more copies than all of the others put together, and it's one of my favorites.'

Java Turtle has a lighthearted feel and a highly visual sensibility. Lowe also publishes *Blackgirl Stories*, which is more personal and serious. 'In the beginning, I was going to write about my experiences as a black woman, [but] the zine took a different direction,' Lowe says. 'I wrote about personal stuff like the death of my best friend, dealing with jealousy, and a whirlwind trip to Connecticut. I learned everyone could relate to these stories, and that skin color had nothing to do with it.'[5]

Reaching a larger audience without compromising

Some zines became quite large projects, and although few have ever had paid staff, these became group projects by necessity or by choice. *Maximum Rock'n'Roll* (it now has a web site: www.maximumrocknroll. com), a San Francisco-based punk zine founded in 1981, is the size of a typical newsstand magazine, anywhere from 64 pages long to well over 100. All of the material is either contributed by readers ('scene reports' about punk life in their town, interviews, and sometimes reviews) or written by a revolving cast of volunteers who, in the early days, simply showed up on editor Tim Yohannon's doorstep. As the people involved changed, *MRR* changed – the first group had a greater interest in the artier side of punk than the next, which tended to focus on hardcore punk, and which was followed by others with different tastes. The process of creating an issue was like personal zine-making writ large: volunteers were pointed towards blank page templates, a drawer full of backgrounds and collage materials, and an in-box filled with stories and art that had arrived in the post, and told to get on with it. Amazingly, an issue always came together. A small core of volunteers worked on cover stories and major features, but many of these were reader-written as well.

Yohannon came to zine publishing through his record-collecting habit, which led him to start a community radio show in 1977. Its audience was *MRR*'s original target. He did very little editing in the sense of deciding the magazine's content each month – as noted, that was a semi-communal process – although he was always a forceful and opinionated presence in 'staff' meetings until his death from lung cancer in 1998. Perhaps his most important contribution was that for political reasons, he vociferously resisted the temptation to turn *MRR* into a business. Instead, he kept his day job as a museum porter, and whenever the zine made money he argued that it should be ploughed back into the community. Yohannon's insistence on seeing *MRR* as a community project or a form of organising resulted in large grants of time and cash to the Gilman Street Project, a non-profit club/community centre; to a mail-order service that tried to solve the problem of rip-off distributors; to a record shop that doubled as another community centre; and to dozens of other fanzines that were struggling financially.

Seven years after Yohannon's death, *MRR* is still thriving – and it still refuses to sell advertisements to major record labels.

Trying for an alternative business model

Yohannon and some other 'major' zine-makers actively tried to resist becoming businesses. Not only did *MRR* give away its profits, it published its budget every year to prove it.

Other zine publishers did decide to start for-profit businesses, earning all or part of their income from publishing. Los Angeles-based *Flipside* (now defunct) went in that direction, as did *Hip Mama* (www.hipmama.com). Still others took the skills they gained in the zine world and applied them to larger, more professional endeavours. For example, V. Vale, the Japanese-American editor of seminal late-1970s punk zine *Search and Destroy*, started up a typesetting business and parlayed it into the independent book publishing company RE/Search (www.researchpubs.com), which he still runs from his San Francisco apartment.

RE/Search gave Vale an outlet for exploring his personal enthusiasms in greater depth, and sharing them with others. It also allowed him to make a living from his passion. '*Search and Destroy* was only ever supported by benefits, not ads or sales – it was impossible to get paid for doing a magazine,' he says. Still, the solitary nature of editing and publishing books didn't quite match the excitement of his *Search and Destroy* years. 'Back then I was more connected, I had a much larger network socially, internationally even,' Vale says. 'I was part of a kind of zeitgeist and I was out there trying to promote that. It was a collaborative, social project. I wasn't particularly happy about transitioning into the books, because it was more of a "me me me" kind of thing.'

Vale's interest in the surreal and unusual led to a few titles that sold quite well. RE/Search's *Modern Primitives* was the first serious examination of piercing, tattooing, and other body modifications, and *The Industrial Culture Handbook* covered the post-punk industrial music scene when it was still in full swing. The topics he has chosen are those that excite people enough to create a subculture around them, so it's still that connection with the social that moves him. 'All undergrounds are the same,' Vale says, quoting the artist Bruce Connor. 'Superficially there's these surface changes, but it comes from the impulse to form your own society, to be more creative. It's nothing about the profit motive or exploiting your friends.' Asked if he's ever been tempted to do a book strictly for commercial gain, he claims it has never entered his mind: 'I have so many projects I want to do, I'll never be able to finish them before I'm dead,' he says.

What has changed is the publishing environment, he cautions. 'It's a struggle these days, independent publishing. The generic problem is an absolutely fragmenting and imploding attention span, caused by the takeover of people's consciousness by electronic media, especially television. We are in an atmosphere, an immersive environment, through television, the internet, street signs – we're inundated with a huge mass of emotionally overwhelming brand names, and it's too much to process.'

Vale's response to the incredible shrinking attention span has been to meet his readers halfway. He aims for a fifth-grade reading level whenever possible ('that's the age I was when I started reading heavy-duty material', he notes) and high-quality, large photos have always been a key element of RE/Search books. Recent titles have included books of quotes, and he finds books of interviews increasingly attractive because, he says, 'people are forced to be accessible in conversations.'

One of his goals is to preserve the art of conversation, Vale says, adding that he means 'the kind that's really lengthy, not hacked into lots of sound bites. Real conversation is almost *about* digression,' he says. 'I follow the idea of the "third mind" that I got from [Brion] Gysin and [William] Burroughs, that whenever two people are talking you have this "third mind" where between you an idea is generated, something new that you've created together, not just rehashing some part of your biography or current events.'

One of the greatest challenges he faces is the frankly bizarre nature of modern book sales. 'This is the only business where years later you can return [merchandise] even without an invoice number attached,' he says. 'There's no other business that has this thing of unlimited returns, no permission required.' Chain bookstores are among the worst offenders, and their spread has put thousands of small shops that carried specialised and used books out of business. This means people are less likely to encounter new ideas, Vale fears. 'In my last interview with [author] J. G. Ballard, we were talking about how both of us spent our early years in bookstores all the time,' he says. 'What a used bookstore offers that the internet never will is the serendipity factor, where you find something you weren't actually looking for and it sends you off in a new direction.'[6]

Personal media goes online

There are fewer fanzines today than there were ten or twenty years ago and, as Vale notes, small, independent publishers face growing challenges. There's still media space for the personal, however, and much of it has moved online.

One of the great success stories of the web is blogging (the name is a contraction of 'web logging'), the practice of putting personal stories and views online where others can read them. Most blogs also contain copious links to things that the blogger finds interesting, from other blogs to digital music files. Some are interactive, allowing readers to comment on what the blogger has written; some are group projects.

Like the fanzine world, the 'blogosphere' is a heterogeneous environment. Although no statistics exist, the vast majority of blogs are probably strictly personal, or relate one person's identity, ideas, and beliefs to the larger world. Like personal zines, these may appeal only to the writer's friends, or to people who are very similar to the writer. Sometimes, however, current events give the personal a much wider appeal.

For example, when a US-led military coalition invaded Iraq in March 2003, blogs written by average Iraqis provided one of the few sources of views from inside that people in the West could access. Mainstream media coverage was constrained by wartime regulations, and concentrated on military movements and politics. Bloggers like 'Salam Pax' (dear_raed.blogspot.com), however, spoke with great candour about their lives while Iraq was under attack, and have continued to do so during the US occupation.

For example, 'Najma Abdullah', a 16-year-old girl from Mosul, Iraq, started publishing her blog, 'A Star from Mosul' (astarfrommosul. blogspot.com), in 2004. Her daily posts are at times reminiscent of *The Diary of Anne Frank* – a very teenage mixture of worrying about final exam marks, stories of family and friends, and the war outside her window.

Her uncle, who is also a blogger, introduced Abdullah to the idea. 'I wanted to fill my time,' she says. 'I had nothing to do in the break [from school] and I was really interested in learning about others. Also, it gave me a good opportunity to test my English skills.'

Some of her earliest posts were rewritten entries from her private diary. Because power for running a computer is only intermittent in Mosul, each entry is written out on paper, then typed up and posted only when the power comes on. Most of her readers are English speakers – and none of them are her classmates. 'Some do know about it, but none read it because I'm the only one in my class who has internet [access],' she says. 'It somehow makes me more comfortable. I write stuff that they might not like, and I feel more free to write without them reading what I write.'

Like most 16-year-olds, Abdullah's main day-to-day concerns are not about politics. But in Iraq, politics and military activity intrude severely on daily activities at the time of this writing, so that her entries offer a poignant view of a life disrupted:

> Today, I had a Chemistry exam. The bridges were closed in the morn-ing (And still are), many students couldn't come to have the exams they had because they live in the other part of the city. Some managed to soften the heart of the Americans by crying and came to have the exam but only an hour before the end of the exam; however, they won't be able to go back to their homes. Some others managed to come on foot ... We had the exam at last, but we don't know if we're going to have to do it again with the others later.
>
> It seems like the Americans are losing control on everything. They seem to be shooting everyone in their way. The guard of our school (An old man who has a difficulty hearing, and who has 9 children, and who has managed to work as a driver in his free time) got killed by the Americans with everyone who was in the car with him. My friend's aunt got killed by the Americans too. ('A Star from Mosul', 10 January 2005, text unedited)

Abdullah says that for her, the social aspect of blogging has been the most important part. 'I love to communicate with my readers (the nice ones) and I love it when I get photos or e-cards from them,' she says, adding that she has made many friends through her writing. 'I want to go on with it as long as I can. Maybe one day my own small family will blog with me, and pictures of my children living in a peaceful country will replace the photos of [my niece] Aya.'[7]

Lynne Lowe of *Java Turtle* has also taken up blogging. Although blogs and personal zines may have similar personal content and social goals, working in these media is different. 'Blogging doesn't take much think-ing at all,' Lowe says. 'With blogging my writing is free-flowing. I write quickly and honestly. When publishing a zine I tend to be more critical and picky. It can take months to finish an issue because you are dealing with story ideas, layout, finding clipart or pictures to use, spell checking, and the little things.'

Lowe says she sees her web site as a companion to her print zines, something that helps her get in touch with potential readers who don't have access to the few cafés and bookshops that carry printed zines. She has also set up her own distribution service on her Web site, carrying her two zines and others that she likes.[8]

Why publish? Why not!

There are as many reasons for creating small-scale, personal media as there are reasons to take up any enjoyable or useful activity. Lynne Lowe says: 'I'm usually motivated to by an emotion or an observation. Being passionate about something is often what makes me pick up a pen or sit in front of a computer screen. If you are interested in starting a zine, don't let anyone tell you it's stupid or uninteresting. If you have a vision, go for it.'[9]

V. Vale agrees, citing the deep satisfaction found in expressing yourself and knowing that you have created something of significance. 'In order to get anything done that you're going to be lastingly proud of, it has to reflect your uniqueness, and perhaps one or more obsessions you've been nurturing over a long period of time,' he says. 'I really think when you're on your deathbed the only things you'll be happy about are anything creative you had 100 percent control over, and a handful of loving relationships. Those are the only things that matter.'

Exercises

Think your life is too boring for anyone else to be interested? You're wrong – you don't have to be a celebrity or a high achiever to have something important to say. If only 100 people in the world are interested in that something, great – those are exactly the 100 people you would most like to know. The following exercises are an experiment in hands-on, small-scale personal media creation.

7.1 Make your own zine

The easiest way to make a zine is by stapling together sheets of A4 or 8.5-by-11 paper. You can also fold them in half, creating a booklet: two two-sided pages put together and folded in half will create an eight-page, pamphlet-style zine.

What goes inside is up to you – the goal is to communicate something personal. Ideas include:

- A diary of your days as a student.
- Your opinions on anything from politics to breakfast cereals.
- Fiction, real-life stories, or poetry.

- Stories, information, or how-to instructions about hobbies, crafts, activities.
- Reviews of films, CDs, or live gigs.

You can use a computer to write and lay out your zine; you can use it (or a typewriter) just for writing the stories and then cut and paste them on your pages with graphics found elsewhere; or you can hand-write and hand-draw the whole thing. Think about who your audience is, and what your subject is – make sure you're presenting your information in a way that will reach the right people and do your work justice.

Your zine can be as elaborate or as simple as you like. A few things you'll want to think about are which fonts to use for stories and titles/ headlines; whether you will take original photographs, use other people's photos, or use hand-drawn artwork; and whether there's anything artistic you could do to make your zine really special, such as individually customised covers, hand-colouring, or unusual paper.

Make enough copies for everyone in your class or for your several of your friends.

7.2 Make your own blog

You'll need a computer with web access. You'll also need to set up an account to get your own bit of blogging space, which requires a valid email account. There are several web sites that offer free blog software and space, plus templates and ideas. Three that you might try are:

- Blogger: www.blogger.com
- LiveJournal: www.livejournal.com
- 20six: www.20six.co.uk (Note: 20six supports access via mobile phone.)

These three services have online tutorials, but if you choose a different service or want more detailed instructions, the books by Powers et al. and Stauffer listed under 'Further reading', below, can help.

Have a look at other people's blogs (the three sites listed earlier have links to thousands of them) to see what kind of topics and content you might include. Will your blog be a diary-style, 'all-about-me' creation, or do you want to focus on a topic, hobby, or special interest? You'll also want to think about graphics and layout, because too much plain text is unlikely to maintain readers' interest. Can you take your own photos with a camera or mobile phone? Do you have video clips or artwork of your own that could be digitised? Add links to other blogs and web sites that are on your wavelength.

Pass your blog address out to everyone in your class or to lots of your friends. Alternatively, you could do a live demo of your blog.

Further reading

Atton, C. (2002) *Alternative Media.* London: Sage.

The Book of Zines site (includes print and electronic zine listings and resources): www.zinebook.com

Duncombe, S. (1997) *Notes from Underground: Zines and the Politics of Alternative Culture.* London: Verso.

The E-zine List: www.e-zine-list.com

Farrelly, L. (2001) *Zines.* London: Booth-Clibborn Editions.

Grrl Zine Network: grrrlzines.net

Gunderloy, M. (1989) *Why Publish?* Rensselear, NY: Pretzel Press. Online at www.zinebook.com/resource/whypublish.pdf

Pax, Salam (2003) *The Baghdad Blog.* London: Guardian Books.

Doctorow, C., Dornfest, R., Johnson, J. S., Powers, S., Trott, B., and Trott, M. G. (2002) *Essential Blogging.* Sebastopol, CA: O'Reilly.

Rowe, C. (1997) *The Book of Zines: Readings from the Fringe.* New York: Owl Books.

Stauffer, T. (2002) *Blog On: Building Online Communities with Web Logs.* Emeryville, CA: Osborne/McGraw Hill.

Vale, V. (1999) *Zines! Vol. 1: Interviews With Independent Publishers.* San Francisco: V/Search.

8 'Cyberculture': a study of the latest wave of alternative and activist media

From the advent of newsgroups and bulletin board systems (BBSes, the dial-up precursors to the web) in the early 1980s to blogging, web-zines, and digital mass media in the twenty-first century, alternative and activist electronic media have a long history.

Chapter 2 discussed Downey and Fenton's critique of the public sphere, which suggested that it's not one big public media plaza, but a series of overlapping spaces for the dissemination and discussion of information. The internet makes this theory visual, with literal links between web sites and discussion groups forming interlocking webs of information in virtual space. Groups of linked sites and services within the World Wide Web can be subject-specific, audience-specific, or project-based.

Some critics argue that access to the internet is still limited to elites. This is at least partially accurate, in the wealthy nations of the North as well as the developing South. However, access through schools and libraries, via mobile phones, and through ingenious ad-hoc systems has broadened the internet's reach markedly. As of 2003, three-quarters of the US population had been online.[1] It is certain that this percentage has increased since. Usage patterns in Western Europe are broadly similar. Internet use is also growing at an extraordinary pace throughout Asia, Africa, and Central and South America.

One shouldn't be put off unduly by arguments about access, anyway. Those mass-media products traditionally seen as influential opinion leaders and sites of public debate – primarily newspapers of record such as the *New York Times* and major broadcast news operations like the BBC – have historically been much less accessible to the majority of the world's population than the internet is today. Until recently, they were usually available only to those who were geographically located in specific areas, and they were not open to submissions from 'outsiders', other than through carefully edited letters pages and vox pop segments. The web places these traditional news sources before a far wider potential readership than ever before, makes space alongside them for alternative points of view, and provides a way for new voices to contribute to debates through the publication of discussions and commentaries. If the audience you want to reach is online, then electronic media are a workable option.

Obviously, news sources do not gain equal stature or accessibility simply because they are available on the web. Some web sites are so heavy in multimedia content that viewers using inexpensive computers cannot access much of what they have to offer, for example. Firewalls – software that blocks certain types or sources of information – may also prevent access to all sites. Advertising, off-line brand identity, and the number of sites that mention or link to a specific source all act to guide internet users towards some online information sources but not others.

Despite the drawbacks just mentioned, a consensus seems to be emerging that a new part of the public sphere (some would argue an entirely new public sphere) is emerging through electronic media. It doesn't stand alone – the convergence of electronic, print, and broadcast media means that the web has become a tool for accessing content that may have originated in another medium, from CNN news broadcasts to articles from academic journals or obscure political magazines. Editorial filters help readers choose from and make sense of the dizzying array of information available, just as they do in traditional media.

In his article 'Weblogs and the public sphere',[2] Andrew Ó Baoill examines the role of 'bloggers' in filtering the internet's mediascape. Web logs ('blogs') are sites where people put forth their views, post texts for discussion, host discussions, and point readers towards other material of interest online. Ó Baoill's research indicates that the so-called 'blogosphere' resembles Downey and Fenton's concept of the modern public sphere, and he calls it 'an overlapping collection of conversations' rather than a single entity.

He notes that these new media are tightly integrated with traditional print and broadcast media. Much of the discussion that goes on through blogs (and also through other online discussion areas, such as web-boards and email lists) references and seeks to influence the content of other media formats. Finally, although most blogs are not commercially driven in the same sense as traditional mass-media products are, there are hierarchies of access and prominence at work. 'While the blogo-sphere is technically inclusive – anyone can start a weblog – the propa-gation network serves to privilege some over others (with external relationships a significant factor)', Ó Baoill writes.

This can lead to an atomisation of both information and audiences. Left-wing readers will tend to visit and trust blogs, web sites, and chat rooms that have roughly similar political views to their own, and right-wing readers will do likewise. Although sites on opposite sides of the political spectrum may reference each other's material, it will often be done in a snide or dismissive context, not as part of the free public debate that might characterise a truly inclusive public sphere. That's not so very different from the situation that applies in traditional media, of course.

The best uses of electronic media

Although they are imperfect, electronic media can be useful for alternative media practitioners and activists. They provide ways of reaching potentially large audiences that are much less expensive than any other method, and can provide some types of information that traditional media cannot. For example, an investigative piece can be posted with links to readable pictures of the actual source documents.

One does not need actually to own a computer or have a personal internet connection to access information or publish online – a number of homeless people in the US have published their views through online discussion groups or blogs using connections at public libraries or schools, for example.[3]

Electronic media can also reach widely dispersed audiences who may share a special interest – Autistics.org, profiled in Chapter 3, is a good example of an online publication like this.

Finally, although the internet is not a perfect meritocracy, where the best, most interesting, or most timely writing will always win the most readers, it potentially offers far more space for alternative points of view than the mainstream media.

Alternative and activist media online: a woman's-eye view

The internet has been a vehicle for non-mainstream views and efforts at social change since its inception, fostering interchanges that are both alternative in their non-commercial and open-access format, and activist in their practice. It's interesting to examine how this has worked, but a study of every such effort is beyond the scope of a single book chapter. The following section offers a guided tour focused specifically on women's alternative and activist online media.

The internet began as a network of computers set up by the Department of Defence and the RAND Corporation in the 1970s. This ARPANET, a closed military data network, was eventually opened up to universities, research centres, businesses, and then individuals. It was relatively easy to create computer programs that allowed groups of people to talk to each other electronically. The hard part was adding a human element to this construct that protected the weak from the strong, eliciting opinions and ideas from the quiet as well as the loud.

In some early online communities, like the WELL in Sausalito, California, witty conversation and deep thinking were encouraged. (Originally a dial-up service when it was founded in 1985, the WELL is now owned by Salon.com, and is online at www.well.com.) It relied on subscribers who felt passionate about preserving the feeling of community, and sometimes also on official hosts who acted as moderators. When users were given power over their environment, structures were suggested and adopted that preserved civility to whatever degree the community wanted it preserved. On the WELL, for example, debates could get downright nasty, but forwarding private email to a third party without permission was considered talking behind someone's back, and deemed thoroughly unacceptable.

Its environment felt very different from that of early commercial online services, even those that styled themselves as 'communities'. CompuServe and AOL were useful for doing business and emailing individuals, but they certainly did not foster community-building, activism, or inclusiveness. Early critics pointed to their top-down organisational model, and their overall lack of diversity.

Indeed, one big difference between these two kinds of systems was immediately obvious: on the WELL there were women who spoke up, while on commercial services like CompuServe there generally were not. This is not to say that the WELL was home to equal numbers of men and women; there was simply a comfort level and a structure that appeared to be congenial. This made a real difference in the atmosphere. When the environment was right, men often felt safer soliciting the opinions of women online than they might in the office, where it could be interpreted as weakness or be misconstrued.

If women first experienced computer-mediated communications through a company like CompuServe or on an unmoderated mailing list, it was tempting to avoid electronic media for anything but work. These systems didn't seem to enhance women's personal lives or defuse the power relationships they already dealt with at home and at work – they just extended the same old attitudes into the digital realm. Women's contributions to discussions were frequently overlooked or dismissed. Overtly sexist behaviour, such as sexual harassment, was also common.

As the internet grew, people puzzled over how best to graft its global access to ideas and people into a community structure that was supportive and female-friendly. Those who had grown accustomed to life-affirming online networks like the WELL wanted to know how much larger online communities could be formed that welcomed people from all over the world, yet still had room for the individual voice – and for women's voices in particular.

Programming and power

Rena Tangens pioneered several innovations in online media during this process of discovery. Tangens's //BIONIC BBS (bulletin board system) became the focus of a German computer community. Tangens, a computer artist and activist, became the den mother of the German hacker scene and one of the first people German journalists called when sourcing a story about life online.

However, most of the questions they asked her about women were complete drivel, she says, the same old cybersex/cybersleaze/cyber-harassment triangle that defined the majority of writing about women online in the 1990s. Even when she was interviewed for a serious article, the editors insisted on decorating it: a photo of a cute blonde model sitting on a terminal and captioned 'Ich bin eine digitale Frau' ('I'm a digital woman') led off a January 1996 story for the German magazine *Amica*, for example.

What Tangens really wanted to do was put women in control of their own destiny in the new online world. The problem, she insists, wasn't getting women simply to be *present*, a fact too often ignored by campaigners for women's access to computer networks or job opportunities in the computer industry. Tangens argues that activists must determine for themselves what goals they wish to achieve with (or without) technology, rather than passively allowing the medium to manipulate their actions. To make it work differently, it has to be redesigned.

'The first thing you have to ask is, whose biology and psychology is being programmed into these machines?,' Tangens asks. 'Is there a gender bias to the choices made?'

Many computer systems simply replicate existing power relationships between experts and individuals, such as medical advice programs that keep patients in a passive role, and 'smart' surveillance systems that keep track of citizens' movements. Could systems be designed to foster cooperative work? And what about the PC on your desk, the email system in your office, or even the internet itself – whose beliefs and desires shaped these tools, and how do they in turn shape and control the end users?

The answers to such questions can be disquieting. 'For example, in one BBS program's administration module when you log the users there's a box where you could tick "female" – "female" is an additional feature, where male is normal,' Tangens fumes. '"Female" as a special feature is just documenting the thinking of the programmer. And the way we communicate is highly channelled by the software.'

When you get right down to it, Tangens is not even too sure about the nature of binary logic itself, the on-off circuit concept that all computing is based on. 'There you have a manifestation of a binary view of the world: 1 and 0. This is the way you talk about male and female, technology and nature, logic and emotion. It's an open question whether a system like this can be as complex as real life.'

She's not cogitating in a vacuum here. An entire body of feminist analysis concerning dichotomous systems has sprung up, much of it centred on the American journal *Signs: Journal of Women in Culture and Society*. Since at least the mid-1980s, scholars have been teasing out the use of false or misleading dichotomies in science: objective/subjective, culture/nature, and reason/emotion, to name just a few.[4] These dichotomies form the basis of scientific classification as we know it and, these scholars reason, have been used largely to make male domination and authoritarianism in general appear to be 'scientific'.

Most of the articles and studies to date have concerned the social sciences, because it's our social role that most intimately defines what it is to be a woman, perhaps even more than biology. Some theorists have concerned themselves with the medical sciences, while a few, like sociologist and psychologist Sherry Turkle, are extending the same analytical tools into the computer world. The only way to change the situation, Tangens says, is to keep asking those questions, look for the answers, and work like mad to find a route around the dominant paradigm.

You've got to start by being 'nosy', as Tangens puts it – get comfortable with the equipment, play with it, see just how far you can make it go. In the computer world this is called 'hacking'. But although the original hackers were computer explorers in academic labs, the current crop of boy nerdlings seems to have reconceived it as a heroic endeavour – the better to let men who sit at a computer all day instead of pounding steel or hunting feel properly macho. They trumpet their deeds in Homeric style, laying them down as a challenge to any upstart coder who follows. It's a game of one-upmanship, and although hackers do share tips and tricks, although they even form clubs and 'gangs', the accent is still on the individual.

But faced with a potentially life-or-death dilemma, and perhaps informed by a tad more education and better social skills than the average teenage geek can muster, German hackers joined up with Rena and other politically active women in an unprecedented collaboration.

It's a story that offers hope to those who want to believe that mechanisms intended to control can be used for human ends, and it was one of the first to explore the subversive possibilities of the internet as alternative media.

A nuclear reaction

The catalyst was Chernobyl, the 1986 Russian nuclear accident that alone generated the creation of politicised underground electronic media in Germany. The Russian government was claiming that it was just a minor incident, but radiation monitors in Scandinavia were picking up hints of something much worse. The anti-nuclear grapevine was buzzing with stories about a disaster with deadly ramifications. Had there been a meltdown? Which way was the radiation moving? Were the tales of massive evacuations true?

Maybe high-level European government ministers had been briefed, but the information was not getting to the people – quite possibly deliberately, to avoid a public panic. Mainstream publications were also being cautious, and the alternative press couldn't get information into print fast enough to keep pace with breaking developments, most of them being relayed via unofficial channels.

The Atari computer that Tangens used to handle her art-gallery mailing list turned out to be her key to bypassing the barriers. She became part of a group of young Germans who piggybacked a new, instantaneous information network onto the tiny existing BBS networks in Germany and throughout Europe.

At first, they tried to use FidoNet, a low-tech computer networking system designed by American anarchist hacker Tom Jennings. His free software package, Fido, let callers post information and send email among users on a dial-up BBS; FidoNet allowed the whole world of Fido-using computers to exchange files and messages, bouncing them over modems from one Fido machine to the next until all reached their eventual destinations, including machines linked to the larger internet.

Jennings intended FidoNet as an experiment in uncensored communication, but in Germany the FidoNet network was run by computer hobbyists whose attitude to requests to carry politically charged radiation alerts was less than positive: 'Basically, it was "keep your terrorist information off our network",' Tangens says.

An alternative route was needed, so the Zerberus mailbox (BBS) software package was created, and Z-Netz, a network of Zerberus-using BBSes that eschewed the heavy-handed hierarchy of Germany's FidoNet, came into being. Activists also made use of other nascent networks.

The result was rapid and wide dissemination of the real Chernobyl news across Europe and then the world. If erroneous information was reported one day, multiple researchers could rebut it instantaneously. Traditional journalists worked furiously to get up to speed with this new medium, while activists like Tangens revelled in its immediacy. Although eventually the Chernobyl crisis faded, the network built to respond to it did not. Unlike hackers working in the heroic mode, the hackers behind Z-Netz and its companions did not move on to the next contest. They have become a permanent part of the European political scene, expanding their reach constantly to meet new challenges, like war in the Balkans and political censorship at home.

Tangens contributed heavily to Zerberus, not only writing the user and systems operator handbooks but also insisting that encryption and other privacy guards be included as a standard feature. Female Z-Netz users especially appreciated little niceties like the anti-harassment feature that let you reply to any message from an online idiot with a standard form like 'Your message with subject <blah-blah> has been ignored by <name>'. Persistent jerks could be permanently tagged to merit such replies: they'll keep on getting the same message until they finally 'get it'.

Like many programmers, Rena sees the design of software as an art form, although as a professional artist she's a bit more literal about it than most. 'This is part of my artwork,' she says about her //BIONIC BBS. 'I designed a "room" something is to happen within.' The //BIONIC BBS and the larger Z-Netz project were like a performance artist's installation, with audience participation taken to the utmost. And although she doesn't believe that differences in how men and women see the world and move within it are biologically determined, Tangens feels that building in support for traditionally 'female' roles like nurturing, supporting, and cooperating is vital to making computer networks serve humans, instead of serving us up on a plate for the technocrats' lunch.[5]

Tangens's online world is a safe space for both sexes. Not perfect, not sanitised of controversy, ill will, or sexism, but equipped with tools and processes that empower people to help themselves and reach out to others for help. Psychologist and author Carol Gilligan, in *In a Different Voice*, has said that her female research subjects described their world to her as 'comprised of relationships rather than people standing alone, a world that coheres through human connection rather than systems of rules'.[6] This description differs somewhat from the more competitive and individual-centred model of the world that men have described in similar studies. Computer communities like //BIONIC and the Z-Netz system have attempted to extend this collective/cooperative world-model into cyberspace.

Building a digital home

When asked what a literal 'home' in cyberspace might look like, one of the web architects Tangens referred to was Marleen Stikker. While //BIONIC and Z-Netz were a world described mostly with words, Stikker's vision was both content-rich and intensely visual. As the founder and, for awhile, burgermeister (mayor) of Amsterdam's De Digital Stad (The Digital City: www.dds.nl), she became something of a cyberspace Corbusier.

Unlike the visionary French architect and urban planner, however, she's not one to impose her own utopian ideals on a passive population. De Digital Stad owed a closer debt architecturally to Paolo Soleri's Arcosanti, the experimental eco-city built in the Arizona desert: although the project was based on community-centred values and hopes, it was envisioned as forever changing. The process of organic change initiated by individual users or small groups was built into its system, ensuring that De Digital Stad would be shaped by its own inhabitants as much as by its original designers or current technological managers. This system reduced the level of central control, building in the possibility of spontaneity and making it less likely that users' interactions will be covertly or overtly controlled.

From an office in what is undoubtedly the lightest, airiest, most comfortable castle turret in Holland, Stikker applies her considerable skills to making technology serve the people, as director of the Waag Society for Old and New Media. She's a hacker, in both the broad and specific senses of the word: a person who tries to get the most out of tools, examining processes and trying things that haven't been done before. In fact, it was at a hackers' conference that she and a few friends began to make real her idea of an online city, complete with virtual buildings, public squares, and entertainment venues. In this digital city, Stikker declared, electronic communications would be a factor for bringing the citizenry together, not a means of isolating them from each other behind their keyboards and screens.

At the time Stikker was working at Amsterdam's De Baile, a centre for avant-garde and left-wing arts that also featured a popular bar and café. During her tenure, the whole building became a 'magazine' called *Live*. 'There was debate, discussion, and some computer-mediated communications – a dating service via phone mailbox,' she explains. She was also working with Free Press Now, an Amsterdam-based organisation fighting censorship and propaganda in the former Yugoslavia. This work relied on a burgeoning network of underground BBSes linking Eastern Europe with the West, a network which ran directly into Tangens' //BIONIC BBS.

Seeing what computer communications could contribute to artistic expression and how it could enhance political activity elsewhere was inspirational. That inspiration caught fire at 'Hacking at the End of the Universe'. This was a three-day camp-out in August 1993 where hackers and friends from at least fifteen countries gathered together in tents and an open field to share tips, techniques, and an explicitly socio-political view of hacking. 'It was a good occasion to talk to people and see what they thought of my ideas,' says Stikker. She found that the Dutch inter-net service provider XS4ALL, an outgrowth of the Hack-Tic hackers' club, was interested in working with her and De Baile on the project.

'I thought that was a great combination: a sophisticated cultural and political institution like De Baile and a hackers' community like XS4ALL,' she says.

She even managed to get the Amsterdam city council interested, as it was around election time. 'I convinced them that it could be helpful in communicating with politicians and citizens.' Her vision of an inclusive community – not just computer nuts, not just the Amsterdam counter-culture, but average Dutch people from all walks of life – was persuasive.

And so it was that the Hack-Tic crew, comprised of Holland's most infamous hackers, went to work in the city's town hall, spending part of 1994 connecting public databases to the other resources of De Digital Stad.

Unlike some other attempts at free public networks, which tended to attract only the most computer-savvy citizens, De Digital Stad was an immediate mainstream success. Between 30,000 and 40,000 citizens registered early on for De Digital Stad-based email accounts and cruised the system, which included spaces where users could create 'squares' (public spaces) and 'houses' (semi-private spaces), a MOO (interactive game) space called *The Metro* for interactive fun and conversation, as well as other areas for carrying out projects on their own initiative. By 2000, the system had over 160,000 subscribers.

De Digital Stad was never some manicured cyber-suburbia along the lines of AOL, with discourse sanitised by dirty-word filters and profes-sional forum managers. It was not 'a homogeneous community', says Stikker. 'A big myth of the internet is denying the differences between us: people want it to be the invention of the end of the twentith century, so we can all be one big happy family again.'[7]

It was not merely a forum for high-minded conversation and political debate, either. As in the real city where it's located, people were making alliances, having sex, fighting, and creating private circles of friends. Nevertheless, there was enough cohesion so that when outsiders attacked, the citizens could form a posse with the best of them.

When the Church of Scientology convinced the Dutch government to raid XS4ALL and a private home over alleged copyright violations regarding the church's so-called 'scriptures', De Digital Stad's denizens held a town meeting, and hit the ground running. Actions were planned and carried out, including printing embarrassing Scientology teachings on T-shirts and wall posters, organising demonstrations, and lobbying the government. Meetings were organised to support the defendants, and eventually the Scientologists were forced to back off.

It was a heady taste of power. De Digital Stad became a home for alternative points of view. Independent exposés of government malfeasance were made available along with more mainstream views; left-wing manifestos competed for attention with stolid government studies and right-wing ravings. With the Dutch government cracking down on past centres of activism, particularly the squatting movement, the intellectual action seemed simply to have moved into cyberspace.

Users literally had the run of the place, and that's what made it a vibrant environment. They could write scripts to enhance their privacy or just improve the appearance of their preferred hang-out. 'The idea was for people to be not just consumers of technology, but also creators,' Stikker says. The further goal was that humans should not be *consumed* by the technology, but enriched by it.

Like many other alternative media projects, De Digital Stad changed beyond recognition over time. At the height of its expansion in 2000, its weak internal structure allowed a few members to turn it into a business that earned much of its money from IT consultancy. The old community spirit eventually moved on to other venues.[8] However, it had also inspired people far beyond the city of Amsterdam.

Barbara Ann O'Leary's Virtual Sisterhood, a tool for feminist organising that wired up women's groups in the 1990s, is one example of how electronic media have migrated from elites to the grassroots. (Virtual Sisterhood itself has since spun out into many separate projects, some of which are linked at www-unix.umbc.edu/~korenman/wmst/links_ per.html. It no longer exists as an individual site.)

O'Leary's work began with a non-governmental organisation (NGO), the Women's Environmental and Development Organization. Its job was putting the goals of women's grassroots activism on the UN agenda in time for the Beijing UN World Conference on Women in 1995. 'We did an amazing amount of work with [the UN] over three years to actually make the governments agree with some of the things we advocated, and it was really hard to do that on a small budget,' she says. 'We had an email account at the office, but no one knew how to use it. But when we activated it, we discovered that a lot of people did have email access. In fact, some women in [the Southern hemisphere] were aggravated with partners in the North who wouldn't get on email! Using faxes is very expensive, especially in Latin America.' O'Leary took her cue from them, jumping into action as an advocate for realising the internet's potential as a tool for social change.

With help from the Association for Progressive Communications (APC: www.apc.org), an international organisation at the forefront of global networking for NGOs and activists, O'Leary helped to set up a communications network on the ground in Beijing. The intention was to circumvent Chinese censorship of socio-political ideas and information, controversies swirling around its handling of the conference, and to target marginalised women, Third World women, poor women, and women of colour before, during, and after the event itself.

Many networks had been forged at other UN women's conferences, particularly at the gatherings of women's NGOs that brought together the grassroots side of the worldwide feminist movement. O'Leary's idea was to make these networks electronic, so discussions could continue across national borders long after Beijing and subsequent meetings had ended.

The Linkages web site (www.iisd.ca/women.html) was the centrepiece of this effort. In China, organisations relied on 'borrowed' accounts for internet access, since the government decided no new accounts could be issued during the Beijing conference. Working into the small hours, O'Leary's crew ensured that the daily information feed made its way to a web server called Linkages in Manitoba, Canada. From there publications, transcribed debates, and more were grabbed by women all over the world, then disseminated in whatever way made the most sense locally.

The Linkages site carried ongoing forums as well as news from the International Women's Tribune Center wire service, daily agendas of the working groups and caucuses, and immediate voting results from the conference sessions. An early version of the software package RealAudio allowed O'Leary and others to put recorded interviews online, where they could be played back on home computers or downloaded for use on radio and television. You didn't have to wait for the leadership of NOW, the editors of *Ms.*, or the producers of CNN to filter the events and tell you what's important – you could go get it for yourself and make your own judgements.

When China made an attempt both to control the conference's agenda and to prevent contact between Chinese dissidents and NGOs, by moving the NGO side of the conference out to a small town down a poor road from Beijing, these online links became even more essential. 'A fax network and the online network were activated several times a day during this crisis as we tried to figure out what it meant politically, how to react, and how to get things done with two locations,' O'Leary says. And get things done they did: ten years later, the networking accomplished between women's NGOs in Beijing is still reverberating.

For O'Leary, one of the surprises of Beijing was that women in the most unlikely places were already using technology in innovative ways. In Costa Rica, Maria Suarez was working with the Feminist International Radio Endeavor (FIRE: www.fire.or.cr) to broadcast a women's issues show on shortwave, and getting listener feedback via email. The Women's International News Gathering Service (WINGS: www.wings.org), another radio production group, was distributing women's news and views to the entire world, both over the airwaves and, with RealAudio software, over the internet. In China, female dissidents had mastered the art of working fax machines to the max, creating an information network that operated just below the government's radar. In Eastern Europe and the former Soviet Union, bare-bones computer networks (including the Yugoslavian branch of Z-Netz, ZaMir Net) carried rumours of war, hopes for peace, and messages from refugees between areas where direct telephone contact was forbidden.

When O'Leary got home from Beijing, she knew these people needed to stay in contact with each other, and that others like them were out there. APC's services could help, but isolated groups didn't know it existed. Other computer networks were available that she hadn't heard of before. New technologies could help meld existing fax, radio, and mail networks together with the burgeoning electronic ones.

What these activist women from every nation needed, O'Leary declared, was better tools and improved access. As women like Stikker, Tangens, and the many women's NGOs created spaces that expanded the possibilities for activists online, there had to be some way to link them together. As other women searched for technological tools that would help them carry out their local missions, they needed contact with the pioneers who had the know-how and experience to help.

'I knew the APC women were doing this great work, but it was all hidden in the APC system. And there were women doing great work in academia,' O'Leary says. 'Everyone was struggling off in their own corners.' Her solution was Virtual Sisterhood, an internet mailing list for women's organisations that felt like a coffee morning, except that the conversation ran to how IRC (Internet Relay Chat) worked and how to deal with 'spam attacks'. Her list brought women together, and the web site created as an adjunct brought their efforts out in the open.

'I don't know everyone who has created content that's linked [to Virtual Sisterhood's web site], I just want to create a forum or space for exchange,' O'Leary said at the time. Exchanging information was the key to empowerment for the global women's movement, she believes, and internet technology that allows people to exchange documents, pictures, audio, and video files has a huge potential to supercharge that process. 'That gives you links to media in both directions,' she explains. 'You can take stuff off the net and broadcast it, or bring it back in any language.'

Much of the web space Virtual Sisterhood used was donated by politically active women working at large companies. Their 'investment' paid off quickly, O'Leary says: 'I really like to talk – but if you're on the list for awhile you'll see that we do real work – tons of our "talk" is translated into action. I'm not interested in just having a place to chat.' The section of the Virtual Sisterhood site called 'Breaking Down Barriers' proved especially useful, with links to people, books, and stories both online and off. It was divided into sections for circumventing language barriers, assisting with online access, getting training, and sharing skills.

The mailing list worked better for holding virtual meetings and devising strategy. 'Email is more than a "fax replacement",' O'Leary says – it's a forum for 'group decision making, support, exchanging information.' It was used to match up non-profit organisations in need of web sites with volunteer web designers, to pair translators with writers, and to find experts who could help neophytes, always encouraging action over apathetic 'netsurfing' consumerism.

'How do you create and shape cyberspace? Stop thinking consumer, start thinking information creator,' O'Leary says. 'Maximize the internet's potential for women who are organising for social change.'[9]

Tangens, Stikker, and O'Leary are just three of the many women who have contributed to building a particularly cooperative vision of computer communications. They have provided the architectural plans, the software building blocks, the philosophies, and the context for bringing women into their own online. The new digital worlds they have made are both enhanced and defined by full female participation. And they can be extended to people anywhere, creating the possibility of a newly inclusive global discourse that is already being viewed with trepidation by the powerful: new media that is both alternative and activist.

'Gripesites': another face of alternative and activist media online

In the heady early days of the web, no one was quite sure how online communities would evolve. Some, like Howard Rheingold, put forward a populist, inclusive, hippie-flavoured vision (Rheingold was an early member of the WELL and other experiments in online community-building).[10] The business world, on the other hand, saw that online communities could easily be turned into groups of online consumers. In 1996, two of the ten most-visited web sites were non-commercial (one of them was the WELL, and several of the others were owned by new dot.com firms). In 2004, all of the top ten were commercial sites, with 'old media' companies like Time Warner and Viacom replacing upstart online-only firms.[11]

But even as the commercialisation of cyberspace seems unstoppable, alternatives keep appearing. One of these is the so-called 'gripesite': a web site devoted to consumer or employee commiseration and complaints. Most are aimed at one large company, with telephone and broadband companies seemingly favoured targets. Ntl:Hell (www.ntlhell.co.uk) and Radio Shack Sucks (www.radioshacksucks.com) are typical of this genre. They range from being the project of one disgruntled customer with an axe to grind to collaborative efforts with real change in mind. And unlike the mass media, these sites rely on the views of customers rather than corporations, employees rather than bosses.

One of the most feared collaborative gripesites is the US-based FuckedCompany (www.fuckedcompany.com), which dishes the dirt from disgruntled employees across the nation. Lay-offs, company shut-downs, store closings, and idiotic inter-office communications are posted, and anonymous authors can add commentary in the aptly named 'Happy Fun Slander Corner' section. Named to parody the dot.com-boosting magazine *FastCompany*, FuckedCompany doesn't offer much in the way of its own solutions. Indeed, its message boards are frequently home to ugly racist remarks about Indian computer programmers. Maybe all it's good for is letting off downwardly mobile steam. But as a steady stream of insider documents and explosive secret memos finds its way into the sunshine, and traffic to the site grows, it suggests far more subversive possibilities. Certainly corporate legal teams are noticing – the site has been hit by numerous injunctions over the years.[12]

Most gripesites are similar: they are simply a place to commiserate, not an activist resource. As 'Bliz', the pseudonymous editor of the Burger King workers' gripesite FlameBroiled (www.geocities.com/Capitol Hill/Lobby/2645), says: 'You won't change the system. You can, however, do little things to make your days a little easier, like smoking a cigarette when you take out the trash, or buying your lunch first and then punching out on break. All in all, you are there for yourself, not your employer.'[13]

From invective to activism

WalMartWatch (www.walmartwatch.com/index.cfm) could be said to represent the next step up. It's a well-designed site featuring criticism of the US-based hypermarket chain from ex-employees, small business people, anti-poverty campaigners, and anti-sweatshop activists, all brought together by a common enemy. Its funding is from a trade union.

Not all activism-oriented gripesites have significant financial backing, however. Consumer activist projects online can be driven by a single individual's experience or a small group's mission.

The Kaiser Papers (www.kaiserpapers.org) is a case in point. It was created by Vickie Travis, whose father died while under the care of doctors from Kaiser Permanente, one of the largest health insurance companies in the US. 'I had been blocked from a formal investigation by all local governments, who later were proven to have a financial incentive from Kaiser to not investigate the matter,' she states. 'Upon the advice of attorneys and doctors that were assisting me, I was documenting all material that we could locate on Kaiser. At that time no one had a library of material on them.'

Travis turned her growing piles of paper into an online archive, putting transcripts or scanned documents online where all could find them. The Kaiser Papers web site was built around this treasure trove of material, which is of interest to consumers and investigative reporters as well as lawyers. The site's profile grew as it turned up on search engines like Google, and soon Travis was fielding pleas for help from consumers with stories much like her own, and getting assistance from other health activists as well. 'The site has grown as new topics and patterns have become apparent,' she says. 'Also, each time the government has blocked a formal investigation on these cases, we focus on providing the information as to why it happened. That way the general public and the authorities which do use the material can at least educate themselves, and hopefully prevent what we all have had to go through in the past.'

'We didn't plan on this turning into any kind of advocacy in the beginning,' she says. 'What we have learned is that because of travel distances, lack of incentive on the part of government to provide accurate information, and the isolation that victims encounter with these situations, the web is a viable medium for information.'

Figure 8.1 The WalMartWatch web site: more than just a gripesite.

Travis also had no intention of becoming an activist media prac-
titioner, but now that's just what she is, with an online radio show and
other Web sites as well as The Kaiser Papers. Electronic media have
proven to be the right choice for her crusade. 'Kaiser … pays huge
amounts to all forms of the media and does threaten to pull the advertising content if they do a negative article on them,' she reveals. 'The
media is open about this and tells anyone that asks the same thing. Often,
the conventional media is the actual source of our information but they
are barred from using it themselves.' Her site now includes video and
audio clips, as well as a massive collection of documents.

Travis says she knows of many cases where data obtained from The
Kaiser Papers has helped win court cases, confirmed patients' or family
members' suspicions about substandard care, enabled them to switch
insurers successfully, and even saved lives. 'With conventional media we
never know how our words will be snipped and put back together to
convey something that is not intended,' she says, whereas with her own
web-based media 'I have no censorship. I cannot be stopped from telling
the truth'.[14]

From activism to creating alternatives

The best of the consumer sites move on from advocating change to creating real alternatives. CrazyMeds (www.crazymeds.org) is one such site: a forum for people who use psychiatric medications, but also much more. There are plenty of complaints, and not a little advocacy, but the main purpose of the site is person-to-person information and support.

'No one behind CrazyMeds is a doctor,' explains site director Jerod Poore. 'We're all just a bunch of damaged people with way too much experience and a knack for research.' The language and tone are irreverent, breaking through the fear and stigma that many visitors are trying to cope with. 'It's depressing enough just to be "mentally interesting", it helps when the subject matter is made a bit lighter,' Poore explains, adding that 'people remember stuff that's funny, and humor is a great way of making something frightening more understandable'.

The content is split down the middle between individual experiences and data culled from research. The availability of medical journals online has made it much easier for people to find out what really happened in drug trials, for example, or to trawl through reams of marketing material from drug manufacturers to uncover ways they are trying to push specific products. It's the 'Crazy Talk' forums that take the site to a new level, though, with medication users sharing tricks of the trade, warnings, and immediate personal support. For example, one person trying the medication Effexor posted that he had suddenly embarked on a series of uncharacteristic drinking binges. Was there a connection? Several others emailed back that they had the same experience with the drug, and never made the connection. Now that 'side effect' is noted for new users, and may help them avoid a bad experience.

'The biggest benefit is the community centred around "Crazy Talk",' Poore says, adding that online media suit his audience perfectly. 'It's easy to update, readers can see when a page is updated, there are all the links to other sites, and it doesn't cost the reader anything to read,' he says.

Poore's background in zine publishing (see Chapter 7) has had a huge influence on CrazyMeds, he adds. 'The language, the style of writing, my attitude toward HMOs [Health Maintenance Organisations] and drug companies – straight out of zineland,' he says. To make an alternative or activist Web site successful, what really matters is having something to say, he adds: 'it's just like a zine: [you have to] be passionate about your subject'.

Like other alternative and activist sites, coming up with enough cash is an issue for CrazyMeds – though not as big an issue as coming up with the budget for a printed magazine would have been. The trick, Poore says, is to set up multiple streams of income. 'I make most of my money from Google Ads. After that it's donations (enough to pay my rent)' sent via PayPal. Beyond these major income streams, there are T-shirts and software for sale, and an online bookstore linked to Amazon.com, which pays a 10 per cent referral fee for all click-through sales. 'I'm just now getting offers for fixed ads,' Poore notes.[15] These pay much better than Google's AdSense programme (www.google.com/adsense), which provides an ever-changing stream of advertisements matched to site content by computer. Similar advertising programmes are run by several firms. None of them pays particularly well, unless you run a site where visitors are highly likely to follow the ad's directions to click for more information.

Exercises

8.1 Your own community web

How could an 'alternative media' web site be used to bring together critical perspectives that exist in your community in a positive, useful way? How would it be put together, run, managed, funded? Look at the Melbourne, Australia, Independent Media Centre (melbourne. indymedia.org) for one group's idea. How would yours differ or be similar?

8.2 Theorising identity on the web: what are the implications for alternative and activist media?

In her book *Cybertypes* (2002), Lisa Nakamura draws attention to the appropriation of racial and cultural identities online, a phenomenon she calls 'identity tourism'. In electronic media, from multi-player games to chat rooms, 'race is constructed as a matter of aesthetics, or finding the color that you like, rather than as a matter of ethnic identity or shared cultural referents', Nakamura writes. 'This fantasy of skin color divorced from politics, oppression, or racism seems to also celebrate it as infinitely changeable and customizable: as entirely elective as well as apolitical.'[16]

Sherry Turkle and others have also explored the difficulties presented by other identity games online, particularly men who pose as women (see 'Further reading' below).

The idea of feeling liberated from automatic assumptions about ourselves based on skin colour, gender, physical or mental impairment, or age is a familiar cyberspace fantasy. For those creating media products, however, issues of identity can be problematic. Consider and discuss how identity issues might affect the following alternative or activist media, and suggest ways to cope with potential problems:

1. An online magazine for Native Americans.
2. An email list for women who write software.
3. A web site where environmentalists discuss issues and plan demonstrations or actions.

Further reading

Atton, C. (2005) *An Alternative Internet: Radical Media, Politics and Creativity*. Edinburgh: Edinburgh University Press.

Fernandez, M., Wilding, F. and Wright, M. (2004) *Domain Errors! Cyberfeminist Practices*. London: Pluto Press.

Gillmor, D. (2004) *We the Media: Grassroots Journalism By the People For the People*. Sebastopol, CA: O'Reilly.

Kolko, B. E., Nakamura, L. and Rodman, G. B. (eds) (2000) *Race in Cyberspace*. New York: Routledge.

McCaughey, M. and Ayers, M. D. (2003) *Cyberactivism: Online Activism in Theory and Practice*. New York: Routledge.

Nakamura, L. (2002) *Cybertypes: Race, Ethnicity, and Identity on the Internet*. New York: Routledge.

Trippi, J. (2004) *The Revolution Will Not Be Televised: Democracy, the Internet, and the Overthrow of Everything*. New York: Regan Books.

Turkle, S. (1997) *Life on the Screen: Identity in the Age of the Internet*. New York: Simon & Schuster.

9 From the margins to the mainstream

The boundaries between alternative and activist media are not always firm. Similarly, there are times, places, and situations in which these media influence, inspire, and in some cases even become mainstream media.

'Underground' media have a certain cachet. As noted in Chapter 6, they are frequently open to experiments in design, new ideas about writing and composition, and cutting-edge topics. They are also where many young journalists, videographers, and broadcasters cut their teeth – and at least some of these individuals will want to make their passion into a paying career someday.

As the interview with V. Vale in Chapter 7 makes clear, you don't have to leave the alternative sector to get by. Staying small allows 'alternative entrepreneurs' to retain control over both the conditions of their labour and its end product. It can be quite disheartening to see ideas and cultural referents that have real meaning for you turn up in automobile advertisements or on M-TV, having been co-opted by commercial media as signifiers of 'cool'. However, that process is part and parcel of how the mainstream media retain control over audiences and their media consumption habits. Whether you secretly hope to run a magazine with alternative and/or activist content but still get paid, or whether you want to know how to avoid having your ideas expropriated for some mainstream magazine's profit, it's important to understand how and why this process works.

Reflection, recuperation, and *detournement*

The media both reflects and creates social trends. New styles of music, new ideas about journalism, any emerging strain in the social current will engender media products as participants try to make sense of the latest thing, or to tell others about it. This is a core function for much of the alternative press, and the longest-lived publications act as a trust-worthy barometer of either what's hip, or what their readers should know about. Writers and editors at these publications see staying on top of trends as part of their work, and actively promote those developments that excite them, excite their readers, or (in some cases) excite their advertisers. Most of the time, this can be seen as simply mimicking something that has 'underground appeal'.

Even when radical political or cultural ideas are involved, this process goes on, and some would say that this can cause damage to social and political movements. One way of understanding this, borrowed from Situationist theories that emerged in 1950s' and 1960s' France, is the concept of *recuperation*. As Larry Law explains it, the powerful can either divert attention from radical ideas by 'shifting ground, creating dazzling alternatives – or by embracing the threat, making it safe and then selling it back to us'.[1] In other words, they can employ the 'bread and circuses' diversion method favoured by corrupt emperors in ancient Rome, or they can hype something to death, changing it irreparably in the process.

Recuperation isn't necessarily the work of some all-powerful elite conspiracy. Alternative media workers are usually active participants, because of their propensity to reflect and promote whatever's fresh and exciting. Those in the activist media, too, play the game in their efforts to express radical ideas to more people. The alternative and activist press is a key factor in popularising new ideas and formats; indeed, that's one of the main reasons some media products in this category are published at all. With or without the approval of their promoters, however, these ideas are then smoothed and re-used by advertisers and other profiteers.

Recuperation has been codified into an actual paid occupation by companies like Youth Intelligence (www.youthintelligence.com) and Girl-on-the-street (www.girlonthestreet.com). These firms actively seek out 'underground' trends that can be used to make advertising campaigns or high-street fashions look fresh. Dave Eden writes: 'we could be suspicious that transgressive expression merely works as unpaid R&D, creating new desires and subjectivities to be taken up by the culture industry'.[2]

Illustrations of recuperation are easy to find, both in the current media and in media history. One might point to the way the Virginia Slims brand promoted its cigarettes with suffragette imagery and the slogan 'You've come a long way, baby' at the height of the Women's Liberation movement (a collection of these ads is available online at www.wclynx.com/burntofferings/adsvirginiaslims_ads.html. A more recent example is the use of radical political imagery and slogans by hip-hop groups that are not particularly politically conscious, sometimes even juxtaposed with raps extolling the latest fashion accessories and luxury lifestyles.

Recuperative practices act to minimise the impact of radical ideas by simplifying them into a collection of styles and slogans, then placing them in the mass media's shop window alongside other fashions one might choose to wear today. Equated with the rest of the consumer commodities on offer, they lose not only their power to shock or surprise, but potentially their actual meaning. Even when the message is sincere, the environment in which it is presented creates a built-in dissonance, not unlike seeing a 'Save the whales' bumper-sticker on a Cadillac.

It must be said that this process can go both ways. A second Situationist concept, *detournement*, denotes the borrowing of existing aesthetic elements (styles and forms) and using them to carry radical messages that their original creators did not intend. The original Situationists did this by putting their own words in the speech balloons of comic strips and by dubbing subversive new dialogue over existing films. *Adbusters* (www.adbusters.org), a magazine that currently promotes the *detournement*-based practice of 'subvertising', has created many 'spoof' ads based on well-known campaigns by big brands like Nike and Calvin Klein. Although the glossy images look familiar, they've been subtly tweaked, and the text has also been changed to give quite a different message – about how products are sold by making consumers feel inadequate, say, or about sweatshop conditions in shoe factories.

Punk, rave, and PR: a journey through the British music media

Journalist Martin James is a respected music freelancer for some of Britain's top newspapers and magazines, author of several books on musicians and musical styles, and past editor of music magazines. Like many writers in the UK music press, he got his start in the alternative press. With over twenty years in the field, he's well placed to look at how ideas move from that sector to the mainstream.

'I started in 1978 with a fanzine called *Issue,* and in the mid-1980s had the idea of doing another fanzine but with a more high-grade look – this was the age of *The Face*,' he explains, citing the independent music and culture magazine whose designs (particularly Neville Brody's font artistry) defined an era of graphical experimentation.[3] He later started a Nottingham-based fanzine called *Trash City* with a friend. 'We weren't just interviewing bands, but also artists, and the stories were all about us and our adventures. We fancied ourselves "gonzo journalists" like Hunter S. Thompson,' he says. 'I just enjoyed writing. There was no need to represent some underground culture … until I went to my first acid house party. Overnight I was totally turned on by this underground movement that I thought was so exciting, especially since nothing was being media-driven.' In response, James's *Trash City* turned into a new zine called *Overall*, covering the burgeoning rave scene.

Acid house or rave culture seemed to be trying to avoid the way punk was recuperated, he says. 'We were trying to represent this movement not just from the point of view of people jumping about at raves, but also this new DJ culture, artists, and writers. It was about being involved, and it was anti-star. We were saying "we're no different from these DJs and promoters": the whole culture was against watching someone on stage.'

Unsurprisingly, James finds it ironic that *Overall*, the most deliberately 'underground' zine he had ever done, was pounced on by the mainstream media almost immediately. The BBC did a programme on it, and before long he found himself being headhunted by techno record companies to work as a press officer.

Mainstream music magazines were no doubt impressed with the quality and originality of the graphics coming out of this new scene: the multicoloured, computer-generated, anime-influenced artwork was definitely a departure from the punk and grunge paradigm they had copied for the past decade.

James says that stylistically, the obvious moment of mainstream recuperation was when top British magazine publisher Emap purchased the independent DJ zine *MixMag*. 'They tried to keep it in quite a "fanzine" style of writing,' he says, 'but what the media did was change it into a star system again, with the "superstar DJ".' When the competing firm IPC saw that *MixMag* was selling over 100,000 copies each month, it launched a competitor, *Music*, spun off from the dance pages of the much older *MelodyMaker*. 'It was the first mainstream magazine to take on the computer graphics idea and make it into something highly stylised and glossy,' James says. 'They used PhotoShop to make things look very "druggy", with all these little signifiers hidden away in the graphics, talking to the club scene.'

Within a very short time, many fanzine writers (including James) were offered work in the mainstream press. 'The dance music scene had an opportunity to create a new style, and we wimped out,' he says with regret. 'I felt at the time that I was still "on the streets" and hadn't been branded – but within four years I was working on [mainstream music magazine] *Vox*.'

How 'alternative' are the 'alternative weeklies'?

Readers in the US will probably be familiar with an individual alternative (and sometimes activist) print media format: the so-called alternative weeklies. Exemplified by New York City's *Village Voice* (www.

villagevoice.com) and the *San Francisco Bay Guardian* (www.sfbg.com), many of these tabloid-size newspapers had early links to the counterculture. They continue to present themselves as crusading, muck-raking alternatives to the staid urban dailies.

At the time of writing, however, most of the alternative weeklies are part of chains, and little of their content is truly investigative or radical. A few have been taken over by the biggest of media corporations: the *Village Voice* itself was bought by Rupert Murdoch in 1977, and has since been through a succession of corporate owners. The commercial success of the 'alt weeklies' is down to delivering an elusive and highly attractive audience to advertisers: as Sean Elder wrote in *Salon.com*, it's 'a demographic of college-educated people in their early 30s making $40K and up … media money men see the weekly giveaway paper as a reader-magnet, stuffed with classifieds, personals and ads for "massage" providers'.[4]

Typically, alternative weeklies run a mix of local news, some of which is investigative or has a liberal political slant; coverage of rock music, films, and other cultural events; humour and opinion columns; and, as Elder noted, pages upon pages of 'small ads'. Major advertisers range from national firms, such as car manufacturers, right down to local event promoters and theatres. It's such a profitable mix of ads that these papers can be given away free, distributed through music shops, bookstores, cafés, and sometimes pavement boxes. Most, if not all, also publish online.

PDXS: an alternative to the 'alternative'

Jim Redden was working for the Portland, Oregon, alternative paper *Willamette Week* (www.wweek.com) when his editor sent him to an Association of Alternative Newsweeklies (aan.org) conference. The AAN is the trade association for this sector of the US media. 'It was right when the movie *Batman* came out, and I saw that half of them had cover stories on that. It really hit me how un-"alternative" they all were,' he says. Redden, who was also bumping up against the pay ceiling at *Willamette Week*, began to consider his options.

'At that point the first Persian Gulf war was gearing up,' Redden adds. 'My brother was also working at *Willamette Week*, and we were talking about how similar it was to the Vietnam War era, but without an underground media.' With the war in the background as a driving factor, and the fact that Portland was too small for a better job to be on offer in the foreground, Redden decided to strike out on his own: 'I borrowed $500 from my dad and just did it!' he says.

The Redden brothers found cheap office space above an alternative-music record shop, convinced local poster artist Mike King to do the graphics and scenester Tim Brooks to pen a music column, and got to work on their first issue of *PDXS* (the name was a play on the city's airport code, *PDX*). Like *Willamette Week*, the paper was tabloid-sized and produced inexpensively on low-grade newsprint. Unlike *Willamette Week*, it was outrageous, contrary, and controversial.

Although both Redden and his brother had been involved in left-wing politics, he found that the emerging far right was an excellent topic for articles sure to annoy both their subjects and Portland's famously 'politically correct' liberals. 'I saw an ad for an "Impeach Clinton" committee and went to a meeting,' he recalls. 'It turned out to be this hotbed of right-wing nuts, John Birchers, and survivalists. Unlike the left, they had a whole lot of energy and were the classic cranky Americans bitching against the government – and it reminded me of the anti-Vietnam War days, when it had moved beyond the war and on to opposing the government.' Redden sensed that these people were going to make a lot of noise in days to come, and he was right: 'When Ruby Ridge [a 1992 shootout in which Federal marshals killed the wife and son of a far-right survivalist] and Waco [an attack by Federal agents on a religious sect's compound in 1993, in which seventy-four people died] happened, I had some local sources and some background,' he notes.

Over the years, a number of *PDXS* stories gained a national profile, from Rene Denfield's exposés of statistical manipulation by some mainstream feminists, to Redden's own revelations about links between the racist right, Christian fundamentalism, and the rise of the neo-conservatives to power. People read *PDXS* not to see their own political views reflected, although that happened too, but to be irritated, outraged, and occasionally inspired.

Redden also added a nice line in true crime reporting to the mixture, following up on cases that the police didn't have the street-level sources for. One such series put a local music promoter in jail for murdering an employee, and revealed the seedy side of the music industry as it did so.

For this young reporter, running his own paper was a heady experience. 'I was definitely freed up once I went to *PDXS*,' Redden says. 'I wasn't bound by any kind of journalistic conventions. When I got into covering the populist movement and the militia movement, I fell into all the conspiracy theories that were percolating along on the right wing and found out how entertaining they were to readers. Sometimes I didn't even have to call anybody up, just mine the field.'

After eight years of researching, writing, editing, and selling ads for a fortnightly newspaper, however, the pleasures of making fun of the far

Figure 9.1 *PDXS* specialised in wild stories and bold graphics. This 1995 issue covered everything from mind control to media industry consolidation. (Cover: Mike King/Crash Design, © PDXS, 1995)

right wore thin (as did Redden's bank account). He closed up shop, and now works as a lead reporter for a mainstream newspaper, the *Portland Tribune*.

'I've done my time in the trenches,' he says. 'There are those very few people who figure out how to pursue that labour of love and keep the rent paid, but for most of us, when you get real grown-up responsibilities, like children, you can't afford that any more.'

However, Redden makes it clear that alternative publishing, even if it has a political edge, is not necessarily uncommercial. 'Probably the best example I can think of is *Rolling Stone*, which started as an anti-establishment newspaper and, under the money-hungry leadership of Jann Wenner, is little more than a slightly hipper version of *People* magazine.' Those who don't want to follow in the footsteps of Wenner, who has been roundly criticised as a 'sell-out' for taking *Rolling Stone* away from its roots, should consider staying small and cultivating a variety of income streams. *PDXS* relied heavily on its uncensored small ads and regular adverts from music promoters; other publications may be eligible for grant funding. Filmmaker Michael Moore, who got his start in journalism by founding the alternative weekly the *Flint Voice* (later the *Michigan Voice*), kept his venture alive by convincing musicians to do benefit concerts.

Even reporters at mainstream publications can get stories into print that they might not have thought possible, Redden adds. 'A real basic rule is this: mainstream publications need stories to prevent the ads from bumping into each other, and writers are always under pressure to come up with them,' he says. 'Young writers especially frequently read the "underground" press, either because they have radical political leanings or are just plugged into the zine and shock cultures. This produces many opportunities to write a story based on the fringe ideas, even if it's just a "kids these days" type of story.' Even at the *Portland Tribune*, which toes a middle-of-the-road political line, Redden has been able to convince his editors to run a hard-hitting series about police spying on political activists, an interest he first explored in *PDXS*.[5]

Does success spoil the alternative press?

Redden's citation of *Rolling Stone*'s metamorphosis under Jann Wenner, and his critique of existing alternative weeklies, bring up an important topic: does commercial success, or even mere financial viability, always turn alternative and activist publications into something else?

Independent researcher Bob Feldman questions the reliance of many well-known alternative and activist media outlets on grants from foundations and charitable trusts – many of which have connections with the very institutions one might expect these media outlets to examine and criticise. Although Feldman (see www.questionsquestions.net/gate keepers.html) treats all such funding links as proof positive of a conspiracy to suppress the truth, it's worth examining where the money comes from to do this work, as well as where it goes. Whether your money comes from foundation grants, advertisers, or somewhere else, funders can exercise control over content. Sometimes it's a direct influence, as in the case of advertisers that threaten to pull their ads over certain kinds of articles. Other times it's a more insidious effect, where worries about getting enough cash cause publishers to censor themselves or pander to potential funding sources.

The look and feel of alternative and activist publications are almost invariably reflected or recuperated by mainstream media. In recent years zines and e-zines have been adopted by commercial firms as a marketing strategy.[6] Blogs purportedly by corporate execs are fairly common (and probably written by their PR representatives).[7] 'Viral ads' (advertisements disguised as entertainment, intended to be spread by word of mouth) are actively downloaded because most people assume they are jokes (see www.snopes.com/photos/commercials/vwpolo.asp for an interesting discussion of the viral ad phenomenon). Many people watch MTV completely unaware that music videos are commercials in the guise of art.

And it's not just businesses that can use alternative and activist media tools in the pursuit of divergent goals. In *America's Right Turn: How Conservatives Used New and Alternative Media to Take Power*, right-wing media mogul Richard Viguerie makes a solid case for his assertion that right-wing blogs, web sites, and religious media (which are, after all, a form of 'alternative media' in that they serve an audience that the mass media generally does not) were largely responsible for putting the Bush administration into office in the US.[8] The appearance of being new and fresh, the cachet of appearing to be 'underground', can even be appropriated by the most conservative and traditional elements of society when it fits their needs.

Does this mean that resistance is futile? Perhaps not.

After lamenting the 'wrong turn' taken by early rave/acid house media, Martin James noted that at the time of writing a new form of media has appeared in the dance music scene that seeks only to build community, not to popularise the genre to the mainstream public. 'It's on the internet now, preaching only to the converted,' he says. 'They're not interested in the critics, only in each other – and it's incredibly creative, really fertile ground where some exciting things are happening.'

Looking inward, 'preaching to the converted', is just one way to protect what's most important about a chosen media form. Other strategies have emerged at various times, and will no doubt continue to do so.

Exercises

9.1 Recognising recuperation

Blogging (see Chapter 7) was originally seen as a way of presenting a highly individual view – more of an open personal journal than journalism. As blogging has risen in popularity, however, mass-media companies have tried to attach themselves to the phenomenon in various ways. Working in three groups, have a look at the following three blogs:

- 'Gretawire: Nuts and Bolts' (Fox TV): www.foxnews.com/story/0,2933,146734,00.html
- 'Guardian Unlimited Onlineblog' (*Guardian*): blogs.guardian.co.uk/online
- 'Kristof Responds' (Nicholas Kristof, *New York Times*): www.nytimes.com/kristofresponds

Answer the following questions:

1. In what ways are these blogs part of, or an extension of, traditional journalism?
2. In what ways do these blogs deliver what readers seemed to crave from the original, independent blogs: a fresh point of view, an individual and uncensored voice, and/or a free forum for public debate?
3. In what ways could these blogs be said to be recuperating 'real' blogs, simulating what they do but delivering only the surface appearance, not the content? Why do you think so?

9.2 A look at the alternative weekly model, and beyond

In this exercise we will discuss the financial structure and working/management structure for a hypothetical alternative local paper.

1. Where will the money come from? Your choices include, but are not limited to:

   major national advertisers
   local advertisers: mainstream (retail shops, car dealers, etc.)
   local advertisers: controversial (strip clubs, drug paraphernalia, etc.)
   'small ads': mainstream (classifieds, romance personals, etc.)

'small ads': controversial ('uncensored' personals, etc.)
foundation grants
wealthy investors
subscriptions
retail sales: mainstream (newsstands, bookstores)
retail sales: controversial ('head shops', tattoo parlours)
street sales
targeted individual sales (at rock concerts, etc.)
donated labour or materials
benefit concerts or events
direct fundraising from readers and sympathisers
product sales (T-shirts, mugs, etc.)

Discuss how each choice might impact the ability of the paper to cover certain topics.

Discuss how each choice might impact on the ability of the paper to reach a wide local audience.

Discuss any ethical concerns that each choice presents.

Can you think of other financial decisions that might exercise an influence over content or work practices?

2. How might work be structured differently at this prospective alternative weekly? Journalists are familiar with two major ways of earning a living through media work: as freelancers, selling articles to a media outlet or corporation, and working as employees within a media outlet or corporation. In both cases, there are clearly defined employee–employer roles. Within typical media corporations, hierarchical structures are the norm, with salaries, and even the freedom to undertake or commission more 'interesting' assignments, dependent on one's position within that hierarchy.

How might our hypothetical alternative local paper structure itself differently, perhaps in a way that fits with activist goals as well?

What positive and negative aspects of these proposed structures can you identify?

Further reading

AltWeeklies.com – news and art reporting from more than 100 alternative weeklies is archived at this site: www.altweeklies.com
Association of Alternative Newsweeklies: aan.org/gyrobase/aan/index
Common Dreams' US Alternative Weeklies Archive: www.common dreams.org/weeklies.htm

Draper, R. (1990) *Rolling Stone Magazine: The Uncensored History*. New York: Doubleday.

Fountain, N./Comedia (1989) *Underground: The London Alternative Press, 1966–74*. London: Routledge.

Frankfort, E. (1976) *The Voice: Life at the Village Voice*. New York: Morrow.

Guerrilla News Network: www.guerrillanews.com

McAuliffe, K. (1978) *The Great American Newspaper: The Rise and Fall of the Village Voice*. New York: Scribner and Sons.

Palast, G. (2004) *The Best Democracy Money Can Buy*. New York: Plume Books.

10 New directions for a new century

The tools for creating media have never been more accessible, mobile, or inexpensive – and yet the mass media has never been more expensively produced or less accessible to the average person. What possibilities does this create for alternative and activist media? It depends on whose vision of the media's future you subscribe to.

Many books on alternative and activist media, no matter what era they were written in, look back to some golden age when things were much better. The Comedia group compared the situation in the 1970s and 1980s to the mass radical/labour press of early nineteenth century Britain, and bemoaned the possibility of today's media activists ever reaching such a large market. In the 1980s and 1990s, it wasn't uncommon to hear that the underground press of the 1960s and early 1970s represented the apotheosis of the alternative and activist media, never to be equalled in its reach and radicalism again. And even now, books covering zine culture or independent film look back longingly to the 'glory days' of the 1980s and 1990s.

The truth is that the glory days never were, and never will be unless people who want alternative and activist media to exist get up and create it.

All successful attempts, regardless of time period, have a few factors in common. They are rooted in a thorough understanding of the audiences they serve, and they operate in ways that motivate the media creators themselves. If you feel a great enough need to tell your story, to serve your community/audience, or to celebrate the ideas you want to champion, you will move heaven and earth do it. If your work has the quality and immediacy to grab and hold the attention of your audience, your project will be a success – perhaps not in monetary terms, but in the sense of causing real and valuable communication to take place through the media.

Of course, it's also possible that the prophets of doom are correct. Perhaps tomorrow's media really will be a globalised, homogenised behemoth, owned by a few oligarchic corporations that have been totally successful in squeezing out all other voices. Current developments suggest that if this fate is to be prevented, it won't be sufficient to merely complain. Changes in copyright laws, corporate governance, media accountability, legal regulation, and even audience expectations are driving this trend. Those who care about making non-commercial, community-based, personal, and politically active media will need to take action in the courts, with government media regulators, and with the media-using public to prevent abuses of corporate media power. They must also seize the day, creating new media forms and making use of existing forms that serve their purposes, rather than waiting passively for the mass media to improve itself.

Independent media centres: bringing it all together

The Independent Media Centre (IMC, or IndyMedia) movement offers one possible direction. Chapter 8 discusses events that are part of IndyMedia's roots. Z-Netz, ZaMir Net, De Digital Stad, and similar projects around the world proved that electronic media could be powerful tools for activists. Events like the 'Hacking at the End of the Universe' camp-out and the Next 5 Minutes tactical media conferences that started in 1993 brought together media activists and hackers, particularly those involved in the burgeoning open-source software movement (see www.gnu.org, www.opensource.org, and similar sites).

Sharing ideas about media activism turned to action in 1999, when the World Trade Organisation decided to hold its annual meeting in Seattle. Hundreds of groups representing millions of people around the world wanted not just to protest against the WTO's neo-liberal policies, but to start a public debate about alternatives to privatisation and so-called 'open markets'. It was time to put into practice what a lot of people had been preaching about using the potential of new media to outmanoeuvre corporate media.

In response, the world's first Independent Media Centre was founded to provide an alternative news outlet during the WTO events. The Seattle IMC brought together several video activism groups that had been around for awhile, such as Paper Tiger TV. Online activists, radical journalists, and photographers got involved as well. About eight people signed on as volunteers to run the IMC's day-to-day operations during the conference, but a cast of hundreds assisted with setting up the centre, contributed equipment, or provided on-the-scene reports in every variety of media. Funding came primarily from individual donations, although the group did manage to obtain some limited grant

Figure 10.1 IMC web sites are a global phenomenon, providing news of local, regional, and international events and ideas. (Design: Independent Media Center-Quezon City)

funding (since Seattle, small grants from progressive foundations have become an important part of many IMC project budgets). The Seattle IMC acted mainly as a coordination service for media activists who went out and gathered what they thought was news. Some of these individuals were part of specific protest groups, others were just covering whatever looked interesting. The core IMC collective processed their raw video, audio, and text files, and made these available online. It also published the *Daily Grind*, a print version of the day's news, which was distributed at Seattle coffee shops and at demos.

Although there had been protests at other WTO meetings, the sheer scale and scope of the popular response caught the WTO, its delegates, the Seattle police, and the mainstream media by surprise. Estimates of the number of protestors range from 50,000 to 100,000,[1] with participants coming primarily from indigenous, trade union, feminist, farming, and anti-globalisation groups. Although the majority of demonstrations were peaceful, and even playful, the police responded with violence. As the situation escalated, some properties owned by multinational corporations were vandalised, local criminals took advantage of the disturbance to do a bit of looting, and a state of emergency was declared.

The mass media was caught napping: mainstream reporters on the scene had busied themselves with reporting on the contentious meetings inside the WTO conference (which ended without an agreement), and many were unaware of the much larger unofficial meeting in the streets outside. The Seattle IMC, however, had streaming video on demand, fresh from the streets. It carried eye-witness reports both of the counter-conference that brought together the WTO's many opponents for discussions and workshops, and of the demonstrations in the city. It hosted live feeds from an unlicensed radio station broadcasting from the thick of the action, and cobbled together five quick-and-dirty documentaries from the video footage submitted. Both the audio files and the videos were duplicated for wider, offline distribution.

After the Seattle events, the IMC model spread worldwide. At the time of writing, there are five IMCs in Africa, three in East Asia, three in the Near East, eleven in Oceania (Australia, New Zealand, Indonesia, the Philippines, and related Pacific islands), seventeen in Central and South America, sixty-eight in North America, and forty-one in Eastern and Western Europe. Several more are in the process of being set up.

Each IMC has a web presence, but how it is used may differ on the basis of the people involved. An excellent software package, including a basic web-site interface, is available to all IMCs at no charge. Technical know-how is also on offer, both on mailing lists and in person if needed.

The news values of each IMC collective also differ. Some emphasise environmental news, for example, where others are more interested in other topics. All of the IMC collectives are basically anti-corporate and anti-capitalist in orientation, but a variety of political points of view fit that general description. In addition, the open publishing model used by most IMCs allows any reader to post news and opinions anonymously on part of an IMC web site. A much wider range of opinions gets an airing through IMCs as a result.

News can be posted in any language, and may include almost any type of digital file. Stories may also end up on the main IMC server at www.indymedia.org. This site is mostly a clearing house that leads out to the rest of the IndyMedia world, but it also features a daily selection of 'top' news stories.

A look at these stories provides a snapshot view of how IndyMedia's news values and journalistic practices differ from those of the mainstream media. Even when the topic is one that is also being covered by mainstream news (often, this is not the case), there are significant differences in the sources chosen, the points of view presented, and the level of background research provided to readers rather than simply being summarised. Most importantly, there is far less reliance on the views of Western 'experts' or local elites.

IMCs do not masquerade as objective sources for news: they have an open, clearly stated agenda of advocating radical social change, and this underpins their news values.

Ever since Seattle, stories that originate within the IndyMedia network have occasionally made their way into the mainstream, although that isn't a specific IMC intention. For example, during the October 2003 popular uprising in Bolivia, for quite a while the only news getting out was through IndyMedia. In 2005, it was one of the few news outlets carrying direct news, photos, and videos from Nepal when King Gyanendra declared martial law and shut down all mainstream media.

IMCs are not places where people pursue careers as electronic media specialists or journalists, although many individuals who fit one or both of those descriptions do volunteer with IMCs. Except for the occasional special project that gets grant funding, nobody gets paid. There aren't any IMC 'stars' – you won't see would-be celebrity talking heads in an IMC video, and bylines tend to run small, if at all. Sometimes there are collective bylines rather than individual credits.

Most IMCs are collectives, and the larger network is a bottom-up organisation operating primarily by consensus. Discussions take place in local meetings, on email lists, and through a wiki site (docs.indymedia.org). Wiki is the topic of the next section.

Wiki: an experiment in community writing and editing

A 'wiki' (the term is from a Hawaiian word meaning 'fast') is a web site or other kind of online document collection that allows all users to add and edit content. A full explanation of the technology is available online at en.wikipedia.org/wiki/Wiki and in books like *The Wiki Way*, listed in 'Further reading' at the end of this chapter.

How far can you go with a media form that relies completely on trust and volunteerism? Have a look at *Wikipedia* (www.wikipedia.org), an entire encyclopedia written by contributors in several different languages. At the time of writing, its size surpasses that of the *Encyclopaedia Britannica*, and about 29,000 contributors have been involved.[2] Even translation is done, and double-checked, by volunteers. Many contributors are top experts in their academic, technical, or scientific fields. They compare the process of group editing and revision to the peer-review process used for academic journal articles.

The wiki method has also been used to construct online communities centred on research topics or interests, such as RaisingSocialCosts (www.usemod.com/cgi-bin/mb.pl?RaisingSocialCosts) or Science-Fiction (www.usemod.com/cgi-bin/mb.pl?ScienceFiction). As noted earlier in this chapter, it provides the management interface for the Independent Media Centre movement. Some blogs and online multi-player games are also wiki-based.

The wiki format seems to be spawning some very interesting ideas about online community organisation, conflict management, and cooperative work as well: see www.emacswiki.org/cw for a wide-ranging discussion and a set of documents based on several years of this work in wiki communities.

Is wiki a new form of media? Not really, but it makes the process of contributing to and editing documents more democratic and transparent. Alternative and activist media workers should be able to think of many interesting ways to use it as an extension of current online media forms. The *Wikinews* project (www.wikinews.org) is one effort worth watching.

Portable electronic media

Corporate media think the future is in your pocket, and they hope to be in a position to exploit it fully. Mobile phones can now access email and web content, receive targeted advertisements as you move through a city, and include digital still and video cameras. They are an obvious platform for new kinds of media, as are other portable digital devices like the Blackberry emailer or Apple's iPod.

Free or subscription-based news feeds have been around for several years now, although most were merely functional until better graphics became available. Now products with some of the design features that make print media more attractive and easier to read are beginning to appear. Many newer mobile devices incorporate an FM radio receiver and/or an MP3 player. Technology for downloading and playing video content, whether it's TV shows or feature films, is getting cheaper. You can pick up your email and do a bit of web-surfing. However, most of the content is still just a version of mainstream media.

What might an alternative or activist mobile media look like? Part of the answer is already out there – mobile phones have been and are being used to bring people together, to spread the word about events, and even to create new kinds of events. If you've heard about 'flash mobs', where hundreds of people converge on some unusual location for an ad-hoc party and then disperse as quickly as they came, that's one possibility. The flash-mob concept has moved on from social events to socio-political action: for example, a recent flash-mob event coordinated a mass 'denial of service' attack on fake bank web sites set up to defraud consumers, using both computers and mobile phones.[3]

Digital media theorist Howard Rheingold notes that portable information devices can be used to create what he calls 'smart mobs': groups of people empowered to act together through information received digitally (www.smartmobs.com). Artists can also have fun creating content for mobile devices. Have a look at www.candyspace.tv for artistic audio, video, and images made especially for this new platform.

Podcasting is another way that mobile devices can be used. Any device that can play an MP3 file can run your pre-packaged 'show' instead of a commercial music file or video. A free software package called iPodder (ipodder.sourceforge.net/index.php) can be used to subscribe to and receive these shows (see Lisa Williams's informative video *Four Minutes About Podcasting*, at www.cadence90.com/wp/index. php?p=3548 for more details).

For media producers, it's easy to think of these developments as simply new high-tech tools for gathering or disseminating content. IndyMedia is already making use of photos and video clips obtained using camera phones and video phones; indeed, mainstream reporters and 'paparazzi' photographers are now making use of these tools, since a mobile phone is less conspicuous than even a small camera. Researchers are working on ways to incorporate optical character recognition technology into mobile phones as well (OCR is what scanners use to turn photos of documents into actual editable texts).[4]

However, the ubiquity of mobile devices may also have an impact on the form of media. Media texts could be 'many to many' instead of 'one to many': in other words, the media could become less mediated. Electronic media have put the tools for creating media into far more hands, and as these tools migrate to mobile platforms, many new possibilities may emerge.

Tactical media

For activists, the concept of tactical media has been highlighted in recent years. Critical Art Ensemble (see Chapter 6) defines tactical media as 'situational, ephemeral, and self-terminating. It encourages the use of any media that will engage a particular socio-political context in order to create molecular interventions and semiotic shocks that contribute to the negation of the rising intensity of authoritarian culture'.[5]

Propaganda can be defined as speech or media that attempts to persuade people to take a particular point of view or perform a particular action. Obviously, at least some tactical media might fit this definition. But if you examine the Critical Arts Ensemble definition, it seems clear that unlike propaganda, which tends to involved sustained campaigns, repetitive messages, and coercive (if sometimes benevolent) goals, tactical media seek simply to shift the way situations are viewed, allowing individuals to see them with a fresh pair of eyes and perhaps redefine their responses.

Tactical media projects can range from theory-laden, artistically executed work like Critical Art Ensemble's to providing 'inside information' on controversial topics. The Revolutionary Association of the Women of Afghanistan (RAWA) has carried out political activities under the most dangerous conditions imaginable. It uses a web site (www.rawa.org), audio-cassettes, videos, and print media, such as posters, to reach women in Afghanistan and encourage resistance to the succession of misogynist governments that have plagued the country. All of its media products are tactical; some also fit the definition of propaganda.

'We see the media as a sharp weapon to fight our enemies and to expose their inhuman policies and brutalities,' said a RAWA representative, who has not been named here for her safety. 'In our media efforts, we usually have two main audiences, Afghans and foreigners. Each of them needs different types of media products. For foreigners we try to seek their sympathy and moral and monetary support, while for Afghans we try to show them their real enemies and mobilise them against the enemy. In the past few years our web site, posters, booklets etc. [have] played a great role to raise awareness and funds from foreigners for our cause, while our quarterly magazine *Payam-e-Zan* (*Woman's Message*) in [the] Farsi and Pushto languages was a wonderful tool for our own people.' RAWA has published *Payam-e-Zan* since 1981, with some material also in Urdu. An online version is also available on the RAWA web site.

Media-creation skills are spread by bringing girls from the schools that RAWA runs to participate in the process. 'With the passage of time, these girls learn enough to follow the complete process creating any media,' the spokesperson said.

One RAWA media project that eventually gained wide visibility was its collection of footage showing the abuse and execution of Afghan women. 'When fundamentalists came to power in 1992, and especially after the Taliban banned filming of living things, we saw that this darkest period of our history was not documented by any source and any news agencies and reporters,' the representative said. 'We thought that though we don't have any experience in this field, we will be able to document some crimes of the fundamentalists to be a proof for future and to expose them on an the international level though these images and videos, which are very effective means for this purpose.'

Its film of the execution of a woman named Zarmeena was sent to major Western news organisations, but all refused to run it until two years later, when the US government was trying to drum up support for war on Afghanistan. You could say that RAWA's tactical media became propaganda in the service of other goals.

Figure 10.2 Cover of the December 1998 issue of *Payam-e-Zan*. (Cover: RAWA)

American supporters provided the group with a small mini-DV camcorder with a hidden lens. The camcorder could be carried in a shopping bag, with the lens hidden in the folds of a woman's burqa. After several unsuccessful tries, the group was able to obtain footage of the Taliban's religious police beating women in the streets. The film was smuggled into Pakistan in a box of powdered milk, carried across a mountain pass on an eight-hour trek. At the time, the US government was negotiating with Taliban representatives for oil pipeline rights, which would have further strengthened the regime's financial position.

Releasing the footage was a tactical move to tarnish the Taliban's image among potential investors and political supporters. However, RAWA continues to struggle with the occupation government in Afghanistan, as well as with regional warlords who have similar policies to those of the Taliban. 'We want to tell to people around the world that there has been no fundamental change, women are still captive and pro-US fundamentalists are in power and still brutalize our nation,' the representative said.

The anonymity of online media has been especially helpful, the RAWA representative said: 'Thanks to the internet, we believe we are no longer in a dark corner of nowhere,' she said. 'Our compulsory semi-clandestine situation has not been compromised as we do not have to expose our precise whereabouts and thus invite further persecution.' However, she added, this works only for contact with the outside world.

'Online activism cannot take the place of real-world activism,' she said. 'In our own experience, unfortunately, we cannot hope to use the internet to bring information to our own people. There is no internet access for ordinary people inside Afghanistan, it is very costly and only NGOs and rich people can use it. In many remote areas people don't know what the Internet [or a] computer is. Can you use the internet to communicate with the eleventh century? But it doesn't mean that we have stopped our activities in local communities ... *Payam-e-Zan* gives voice to their anguish, and reflects and chronicles their situation and the fundamentalists' record of infamy.'[6]

Payam-e-Zan is closer to propaganda than to tactical media, as it does seek to persuade people to adopt a specific political stance. As RAWA members begin to take part more openly in civil society within Afghanistan – for example, some now intend to run as candidates for office – it is likely that their skills will be put to work on media products that could rightly be termed propaganda. This is the correct term not because these media products will carry a false message, but because they will seek to persuade people to perform a specific action by voting for their candidates or joining their political movement.

For many people, both politics and community involvement are now an almost entirely mediated experience. Tactical media can be used to ensure that not all of that mediation is carried out from above, and that citizens get the information they need to take part as informed participants. Some forms of tactical media may also show viewers or listeners how to step out of these mediated processes altogether, by facilitating direct individual and group interaction.

A return to community media?

Although it would seem to fly in the face of widely reported media trends, some commentators sense a growing appetite for locally controlled community media. In *We the Media,* Dan Gillmor points at blogs and the IMC movement as harbingers of this reinvigorated local and regional media.[7] Gillmor writes that bloggers and other 'citizen journalists' are making a real difference in how news is gathered, reported, and used. Media created using traditional methods needn't lose out, he adds: among other things, Gillmor has suggested that newspapers connect with these new forms of community media, open up their editorial pages to a multiplicity of voices, and consider moving away from the subscription models that have come to dominate online news archives.

Organisations like the UK's Community Media Association (www.commedia.org.uk), the Alliance for Community Media (www.alliancecm.org) in the US, and Agenzia Multimediale Informazione Sociale (www.amisnet.org) in Italy are advocating changes in licensing models that open up access to broadcasting. Dozens of similar efforts are addressing print and online media: the organisation Global Community Networking (www.globalcn.org) is just one of several. Community media has also been taken up by UNESCO and various NGOs, as part of a general push for recognition of 'communication rights' as basic human rights.

Fighting for communication rights

In the current environment of media law and regulation, communication is conceived of as a commercial operation, not a civic good or a civil right. Laws related to media access, copyright, and even libel are written to protect commercial firms rather than readers, viewers, or citizens – and these laws are having an increasingly large impact on the content of media texts and the dissemination of ideas.

Over the past few years, a growing chorus of voices has advocated an alternative model. Groups like OURmedia/NUESTROSmedia (www.ourmedianet.org) and Communication Rights in the Information Society (CRIS: www.crisinfo.org) seek to make changes in existing laws, and prevent the imposition of further corporate-focused regulations. They advocate increased access to tools for media creation and communications technologies. These efforts have become crucial as new restrictions on non-corporate communication are sneaked in through treaties like NAFTA and GATT, and by organisations like the World Trade Organisation.

The 'Media Carta' (adbusters.org/metas/psycho/mediacarta) has been seen by some as a foundational document in this effort to 'enshrine the Right to Communicate in the constitutions of all free nations, and in the Universal Declaration of Human Rights'.[8]

Imagining tomorrow's media

Just as alternative and radical media pioneers like Ben Franklin and Tom Paine would never have imagined formats like the *San Francisco Oracle* or blogging, we don't have a crystal ball at hand to envision what might come next. The best we can do is look at new technologies and other trends, extrapolating from these in an attempt to anticipate it.

One vision is that 'doomsday scenario' mentioned at the beginning of this chapter, in which a handful of media corporations successfully rewrite global legislation to suit themselves and take over every aspect of mediated communication. They are trying, but many people are resisting. Even if they succeeded, resistance would continue – every act of verbal, in-person communication, every unauthorised leaflet or wall poster, would become an act of resistance. In some places, it already is.

Another vision posits extraordinary changes to corporate media, a sort of hollowing-out effect where many more people (including far more non-professionals, such as bloggers) become media creators. In this model, new forms of media corporations act as brokers. They don't make the news, they channel news made by others to audiences, and they channel advertising revenue towards preferred portals that gather other people's stories. An amusing, if easily contested, version of this idea is presented in the digital video 'Media Museum 2014' (mccd.udc.es/orihuela/epic). Alternative and activist media creators would still have a great deal to offer in this system, but the media would remain an enterprise dominated by commercial considerations.

Other visions exist that are predicated on giving all people access to the tools they need to access, create, and distribute their own media. A grassroots revolution in communication could open up a new, globalised public sphere in which information rather than cash is the currency of choice.

We are at a crucial moment: which route will we choose?

Exercises

10.1 What's different about IndyMedia?

Download the film *The Miami Model* (FTAA IMC, 2004) as a digital file from ftaaimc.org/miamimodel. It can also be ordered on DVD from the web site, or from:

Mountain Eye Media
19 Jarret Street
Asheville, NC 28806
USA

In 2003, IndyMedia activists covering the Free Trade Area of the Americas (FTAA) treaty negotiations in Miami made a documentary that exemplifies the IMC approach. Watch the video, and analyse it using your answers to the following questions as criteria:

1. How is this video different in style from mainstream coverage of meetings like this? What other media forms does it borrow from in terms of style?
2. Whose voices are heard in the video? Are these sources similar to or different from those you would expect to hear in commercial TV network reports on the FTAA?
3. Does the documentary appear to be more or less rigorously re-searched than you would expect a mainstream media report to be?
4. What relationship do the videographers seem to be trying to create with you, the audience? In what ways are you addressed?
5. How do the videographers get their position across? Do you feel that they build up an argument in an ethical way, based on demonstrable evidence, or do they use emotional appeals?
6. Using the definitions presented earlier in this chapter, is this video tactical media, propaganda, or both?

10.2 Imagining your own media future

All too often, when you're learning about journalism, media production, or related areas, you're learning only about what *was* or what *is* ... not what might be. There's a tendency to assume that things will continue much as they are now, even though history offers ample illustrations of ways that the media was different in the past.

In this exercise, you're asked to envision ways that media could change, based on the trends discussed in this chapter and your own hopes and dreams. Discuss the following three questions, individually or in groups.

1. What skills do you think will be essential for media producers over the next decade? How can these skills be extended to the maximum number of people?
2. What are three ways that media activists might be able to get their message across – one for each of the 'visions of the media future' listed in the last section of this chapter?
3. How might laws, regulatory practices, and media business practices be changed to make future media more democratic, honest, useful, and enjoyable?

Further reading

Couldry, N. and Curran, J. (2003) *Contesting Media Power: Alternative Media in a Networked World.* Totowa, NJ: Rowman & Littlefield.

Galatas, E. (2001) 'Building Indymedia' in: Phillips, P./Project Censored (2001) *Project Censored 2001.* New York: Seven Stories Press. Online at www.thirdworldtraveler.com/Independent_Media/Building_Indy Media.html.

Gillmor, D. (2004) *We the Media: Grassroots Journalism By the People For the People.* Sebastopol, CA: O'Reilly.

IndyMedia web site: www.indymedia.org

Lasn, K. (2000) *Culture Jam: The Uncooling of America.* New York: HarperCollins.

Lessig, L. (2004) *Free Culture: How Big Media Uses Technology and the Law to Lock Down Culture and Control Creativity.* New York: Penguin.

Leuf, B. and Cunningham, W. (2001) *The Wiki Way: Quick Collaboration on the Internet.* Boston, MA: Addison-Wesley Professional.

McChesney, R. (2004) *The Problem of the Media: US Communication Politics in the 21st Century.* New York: Monthly Review Press.

Next 5 Minutes 4 (2003) *Next 5 Minutes 4 Reader.* Amsterdam: Next 5 Minutes. Online at www.next5minutes.org/n5m/index.jsp (accessed 10 February 2005).

Powazek, D. M. (2001) *Design for Community: The Art of Connecting Real People in Digital Places.* Berkeley, CA: New Riders Press.

Notes

Preface

1. McChesney, R. (2000) 'Journalism, democracy ... and class struggle', *Monthly Review*, 52 (6), 1–15.

1 Who needs an alternative? An introduction to the role of alternative and activist media

1. Turner, T. (2004) 'My beef with big media: how government protects big media – and shuts out upstarts like me', *Washington Monthly*, July/August. Online at www.washingtonmonthly.com/features/2004/0407.turner.html (accessed 15 February 2005).
2. Hightower, J. (2004) 'The people's media reaches more people than FOX does', *Common Dreams* News Center, 15 June. Online at www.common dreams.org/views04/0615-14.htm (accessed 15 February 2005).
3. Project for Excellence in Journalism (2004) 'The state of the news media 2004: an annual report on American journalism'. Online at www.stateofthe newsmedia.org/index.asp (accessed 15 February 2005).
4. Abel, R. (1997) 'An alternative press: why?', *Publishing Research Quarterly*, 12 (4), pp. 78–84.
5. Atton, C. (2002) *Alternative Media*. London: Sage, pp. 9–19.
6. Albert, M. (1997) 'What makes alternative media alternative?', *Z Magazine*, October. Online at www.zmag.org/whatmakesalti.htm (accessed 15 February 2005).
7. Comedia (1984) 'The alternative press: the development of underdevelopment', *Media, Culture & Society*, 6, pp. 95–102.
8. Rodríguez, C. (2001) *Fissures in the Mediascape: an International Study of Citizens' Media*. Cresskill, NJ: Hampton Press.
9. O'Sullivan, T. (1994) 'Alternative media', in: O'Sullivan, T., Hartley, J., Saunders, D., Montgomery, M., and Fiske, M. *Key Concepts in Communication and Cultural Studies*, 2nd edition. London: Routledge, p. 10.
10. Gutierrez, M. (2004) 'IPS special report – media: alternative and influential?', Inter Press Service News Agency. Online at www.ipsnews. net/interna.asp?idnews=26064 (accessed 15 February 2005).

11. Waters, R., 8 October 2004. Personal communication.
12. Solomon, N. (2004) 'The state of the media union', *MediaBeat*, Fairness and Accuracy in Reporting, 22 January. Online at www.fair.org/media beat/040122.html (accessed 15 February 2005).
13. Ball-Rokeach, S. J. and DeFleur, M. L. (1976) 'A dependency model of mass media effects', *Communication Research*, 3, pp. 3–21.
14. Merskin, D. (1998) 'Sending up signals: a survey of Native American media use and representation in the mass media', *Howard Journal of Communications*, 9, 333–45.
15. Chen, C. Y. (2003) 'Clear Channel: not the bad boys of radio', *Fortune*, 18 February. Online at www.fortune.com/fortune/ceo/articles/0,15114, 423802,00.html (accessed 15 February 2005).
16. Albert, M., 'What makes alternative media alternative?'
17. Ibid.
18. Clark, D., 14 October 2004. Personal communication.
19. *Red Pepper* (2004) 'A brief history'. Online at www.redpepper.org.uk (accessed 15 February 2005).
20. Khiabany, G. (2000) *Red Pepper*: a new model for the alternative press?', *Media, Culture & Society*, 22, pp. 447–63.

2 A brief history of alternative and activist media

1. Harrison, S. (1974) *Poor Men's Guardians: A Record of the Struggles for a Democratic Newspaper Press, 1763–1973*. London: Lawrence and Wishart.
2. Royle, E. (1971) *Radical Politics 1790–1900: Religion and Unbelief.* London: Longman.
3. Randall, D. (2000) *The Universal Journalist*, 2nd edition. London: Pluto Press, p. 23.
4. Ibid., p. 24.
5. Adorno, T. and Horkheimer, M. (1976) *Dialectic of Enlightenment.* London: Continuum International Publishing Group. Online at www.marxists.org/ reference/subject/philosophy/works/ge/adorno.htm (accessed 23 April 2005).
6. Herman, E. S. and Chomsky, N. (1988) *Manufacturing Consent: The Political Economy of the Mass Media.* New York: Random House, pp. 3–4.
7. Harrison, *Poor Men's Guardians.*
8. Habermas, J. (1991) *The Structural Transformation of the Public Sphere*, reprint edition. Cambridge, MA: MIT Press.
9. Herman and Chomsky, *Manufacturing Consent.*
10. Pinter, A. (2004) 'Public sphere and history: historians' response to Habermas on the "worth" of the past', *Journal of Communication Inquiry*, 28 (3), pp. 217–32.
11. Habermas, J. (1992) 'Further reflections on the public sphere', in: Calhoun, C. (ed.), *Habermas and the Public Sphere*. Cambridge, MA: MIT Press, pp. 421–61.

12. Downey, J. and Fenton, N. (2003) 'New media, counter publicity and the public sphere', *New Media & Society*, 2, p. 187.

13. Boggs, C. (1976) *Gramsci's Marxism.* London: Pluto Press.

14. Downey and Fenton, 'New media', pp. 185–202.

15. Straubhaar, J. D. (1989) 'Television and video in the transition from military to civilian rule in Brazil', *Latin American Research Review*, 24 (1), pp. 150–1.

16. Jones, A. (1996) 'Wired world: communication technology, governance and the democratic uprising', in: Comor, E. (ed.) *The Global Political Economy of Communication: Hegemony, Telecommunication ad the Information Economy.* Basingstoke: Macmillan.

17. Albats, Y. (2001) 'Diary of the coup', *Moscow Times*, 14 August, p. 16. Online at www.themoscowtimes.com/stories/2001/08/14/006.html (accessed 15 February 2005).

18. Böök, M. (1991) 'Soviet coup 1991: on-line from the front-line', *Interdoc Europe Newsletter*, 5, 15 October. Online at www.kaapeli.fi/book/coup91.htm (accessed 15 February 2005).

19. Press, L. (1992) 'RelCom, an appropriate technology network', *Proceedings of INET 1992*, June. Reston, VA: Internet Society. Online at som.csudh.edu/cis/lpress/articles/relcom.htm (accessed 15 February 2005).

20. Jones, 'Communications technology'.

21. Welch, A. (2004) 'Stockton truckers join IWW, win 2-Day strike', *Industrial Worker*, October. Online at www.iww.org/unions/iu530/truckers/truck8.shtml (accessed 23 April 2005).

22. Atton, C. (2002) *Alternative Media.* London: Sage.

23. Rodríguez, C. (2001) *Fissures in the Mediascape: An International Study of Citizens' Media.* Cresskill, NJ: Hampton Press.

24. Borton, J. (2004) 'OhmyNews and "wired red devils",' *AsiaTimes Online*, 25 November. Online at www.atimes.com/atimes/Korea/FK25Dg01.html (accessed 15 February 2005).

25. Clark, T. (2004) 'Citizen reporters sound off against traditional media', *Japan Media Review*, 11 April. Online at www.ojr.org/japan/media/1063391165.php (accessed 15 February 2005).

26. Downey and Fenton, 'New Media', p. 199.

27. Enzensberger, H. (1976) 'Constituents of a theory of the media', in: Enzensberger, H. *Raids and Reconstructions: Essays on Politics, Crime and Culture.* London: Pluto Press, pp. 20–53.

3 Unheard voices, unseen images

1. Developing Countries Farm Radio Network (2004) 'Radio for development'. Online at www.farmradio.org/eng/rad_develop.php (accessed 15 February 2005).

2. World Bank Group (2004) 'Infrastructure' (table) in: *World Development Indicators 2004*. Washington, DC: World Bank Group. Online at www.worldbank.org/data/databytopic/infrastructure.html (accessed 15 February 2005).

3. British Council (2003) 'Illiteracy', *LearnEnglish Magazine*. Online at www.learnenglish.org.uk/magazine/magazine_home_illiteracy.html (accessed 15 February 2005).

4. Sen, M. (2004) 'From illiteracy to literacy: change one word and you change everything', *Media Action*, 258, 5 November 2004. Online at www.wacc.org.uk/wacc/publications/media_action/258_nov_2004/from_illiteracy_to_literacy_change_one_word_and_you_change_everything (accessed 15 February 2005).

5. Euromonitor International (2004) 'Executive summary: consumer electronics in India'. Online at www.euromonitor.com/Consumer_Electronics_in_India (accessed 15 February 2005).

6. Greenwald, J. (1993) 'Dish-wallahs', *Wired*, 1.02, May/June. Online at www.wired.com/wired/archive/1.02/dishwallahs_pr.html (accessed 15 February 2005).

7. Poynter Institute (2003) 'The face and mind of the American journalist'. Online at www.poynter.org/content/content_view.asp?id=28235 (accessed 15 February 2005).

8. Pozner, J. (2000) 'Women have not taken over the news'. *Extra!*, January/February. Online at www.fair.org/extra/0001/tvguide.html (accessed 15 February 2005).

9. Tisoncik, L. (1998) 'The original Autistics.org database project proposal'. Online at www.autistics.org/project/project.html (accessed 19 November 2004).

10. Tisoncik, L., 18 December 2004. Personal communication.

12. Marker, J., 14 December 2004. Personal communication.

13. Millington, N., 16 December 2004. Personal communication.

4 Anyone with a cheap transmitter can do radio

1. Dotinga, R. (2002) 'Clear-cutting the radio forest', *Wired News*, 5 August. Online at www.wired.com/news/business/0,1367,54036,00.html (accessed 15 February 2005).

2. Bachman, K. (2004) 'Air America and Al Franken reup', *MediaWeek*, 9 December 2004. Online at www.mediaweek.com/mediaweek/headlines/article_display.jsp?vnu_content_id=1000734720 (accessed 15 February 2005).

3. KPFA (2005) 'About KPFA'. Online at www.kpfa.org/2ab_gen.htm (accessed 15 February 2005).

4. Office of Communications (Ofcom) (2004) 'The licensing of community radio', 17 February 2004. Online at www.ofcom.org.uk/consult/condocs/comm_radio/com_radio (accessed 15 February 2005).

5. Radio4All (date not listed) 'Questions and answers about micro-power radio'. Online at www.radio4all.org/q_and_a.html (accessed 15 February 2005).

6. Federal Communications Commission (2004) 'Low power FM broadcast radio station'. Online at www.fcc.gov/mb/audio/lpfm (accessed 15 February 2005).

7. Ibid.

8. Torrone, P. (2004) 'Make your own pirate radio station with an iPod', *Engadget*, 15 June. Online at www.engadget.com/entry/3597373383872462/ (accessed 15 February 2004).

9. Youngs, I. (2002) 'How the pirates changed music'. *BBC News Online*, 19 December. Online at news.bbc.co.uk/1/hi/entertainment/tv_and_radio/2588687.stm (accessed 15 February 2005).

10. Tridish, P. and Hammersmith, A. (2000) 'The next FCC giveaway: Digital radio'. *Media File*, 19 (4) (September/October). Online at www.prometheusradio.org/artdigital.shtml (accessed 15 February 2005).

11. Australian Broadcasting Corporation (2004) 'ABC Digital Radio'. Online at abc.net.au/radio/digital (accessed 15 February 2005).

12. See the many articles and press releases archived by Digital Radio Australia. Online at www.digitalradioaustralia.com.au (accessed 15 February 2005).

13. Mieskowski, K. (2002) 'Web radio's last stand', *Salon*, 26 March. Online at www.salon.com/tech/feature/2002/03/26/web_radio/index.html (accessed 15 February 2005).

14. Dunifer, S., 25 January 2005. Personal communication.

15. Kelliher, L. (2003) 'Emerging alternatives: low power, high intensity', *Columbia Journalism Review*, 5, September/October. Online at www.cjr.org/issues/2003/5/radio-kelliher.asp (accessed 15 February 2005).

16. Prometheus Radio Project (2004) 'The Southern Development Foundation brings real local broadcasting to Opelousas!' Online at www.prometheusradio.org/opelousas.shtml (accessed 15 February 2005).

17. Mitchell, C. (2004) '"Dangerously feminine?": theory and praxis of women's alternative radio', in: Ross, K. and Byerly, C. M. (2004) *Women and Media: International Perspectives*. London: Blackwell, pp. 157–84.

18. Merlino, D. (2002) 'Mass media for a minority', *Central Europe Review*, 5 (3), 18 October. Online at www.ce-review.org/02/5/Roma_radioKK.html (accessed 15 February 2005).

5 Broadcasting beyond the corporate sphere

1. Fuller, L. K. (1994) *Community Access Television in the United States*. Westport, CT: Greenwood Press.

2. Channel 4 (2001) 'Channel 4's statement of promises'. Online at www.channel4.com/about_c4/promises_2001/promises_intro2.html (accessed 15 February 2005).

3. Indvandrer-TV (2004) 'Info'. Online at www.indvandrertv.dk (accessed 15 February 2005).

4. Higgins, W. J., Jr (1992) 'Minority language broadcasting and the continuations of Celtic culture in Wales and Ireland', in: Riggins, S. H. (ed.)

140 ALTERNATIVE AND ACTIVIST MEDIA

Ethnic Minority Media: An International Perspective. Newbury Park, CA: Sage, p. 217.

5. Johnson, M. A. (2000) 'How ethnic are U.S. ethnic media: the case of Latina magazines', *Mass Communication & Society*, 3 (2/3), pp. 229–48.

6. Interview with O'Connor, P., 3 December 2004. Personal communication.

7. [No author listed] (2004) 'Alamo Drafthouse Cinema to expand nationally', *Movie Marketing News*, 22 July 2004. Online at www.indiescene.net/ archives/alamo_drafthouse_cin.html (accessed 15 February 2005).

8. Messenger, E. (1990) 'Pirate TV in Eastern Europe', *Whole Earth Review*, 68, Fall, pp. 101–4.

9. Berardi, F. (2004), speaking in: Lowenthal, A. *Telestreet* (film). Online at www.archive.org/movies/details-db.php?collection=opensource_movies& collectionid=Telestreets (accessed 23 April 2005).

10. Dean, M., 11 January 2005. Personal communication.

6 Artistic impulses

1. Cohen, A. (1995) 'The rise and fall of the Haight-Ashbury', *Haight-Ashbury in the Sixties* (CD-ROM). Text online at www.rockument.com/webora.html (accessed 15 February 2005).

2. Buchheit, M. (2003) 'A pressing business: a conversation with letterpress guru Bruce Licher', *CreativeRefuge.com*. Online at www.creativerefuge.com/ pages/spotlight.htm (accessed 15 February 2005).

3. Jenkins, M. (1998) 'Artists Television Access opens up tech toolbox', *Metropolitan*, February. Online at www.metroactive.com/papers/sfmetro/ 02.98/video-98-2.html (accessed 15 February 2005).

4. Baxter, E., 31 January 2005. Personal communication.

5. Makagon, D. (2000) 'Accidents should happen: cultural disruption through alternative media', *Journal of Communication Inquiry*, 24 (44), October, pp. 430–47.

6. Ibid., pp. 441–2.

7. Teran, M. (2003) 'Life: a user's manual'. *Impakt Online*. Online at www. impaktonline.nl/life.html (accessed 15 February 2005).

8. Durland, S. (1987) 'Witness: the guerrilla theatre of Greenpeace', *High Performance*, 40, Winter, pp. 30–5.

9. United for a Fair Economy (1997) *The Activist Cookbook: Creative Actions for a Fair Economy*. Boston, MA: United for a Fair Economy, p. 2.

7 Creating media spaces for the personal

1. Waltz, M. (1998) 'Incoherent', in: Gunderloy, M. (ed.) *Why Publish?*, Rensselear, NY: Pretzel Press, pp. 17–18. Online at www.zinebook.com/ resource/whypublish.pdf (accessed 15 February 2005).

2. Gunderloy, *Why Publish?*, pp. 10, 11, 34. Online at www.zinebook.com/ resource/whypublish.pdf (accessed 15 February 2005).

3. Atton, C. (2002) *Alternative Media*. London: Sage, p. 61.

4. Ibid, p. 67.
5. Lowe, L., 7 January 2005. Personal communication.
6. Vale, V., 27 January 2005. Personal communication.
7. 'Abdullah, N.', 26 January 2005. Personal communication.
8. Lowe, pers comm.
9. Ibid.
10. Vale, pers comm.

8 'Cyberculture': a study of the latest wave of alternative and activist media

1. Lenhart, A., Horrigan, J., Rainie, L., et al. (2003). *The Ever-Shifting Internet Population: A new Look at Internet Access and the Digital Divide.* Online at www.pewinternet.org/reports/pdfs/PIP_Shifting_Net_Pop_Report.pdf (accessed 15 February 2005).
2. Ó Baoill, A. (2004) 'Weblogs and the public sphere', in: Gurak, L. J., Antonijevic, S., Johnson, L., Ratcliff, C. and Reyman, J. (eds) *Into the Blogosphere.* Minneapolis: University of Minnesota. Online at blog.lib. umn.edu/blogosphere/weblogs_and_the_public_sphere.html (accessed 15 February 2005).
3. For example, see: Barbieux, K., *The Homeless Guy.* Online at thehome lessguy.blogspot.com (accessed 15 January 2005).
4. Fee, E. (1986) 'Critiques of modern science: the relationship of feminism to other radical epistemologies', in: Bleier, R. (ed.) *Feminist Approaches to Science.* New York: Pergamon, pp. 42–56.
5. Tangens, R., 5 May 1996. Personal communication.
6. Gilligan, C. (1982) *In a Different Voice: Psychological Theory and Women's Development.* Cambridge, MA: Harvard University, p. 29.
7. Stikker, M., 15 May 1996. Personal communication.
8. Lovink, G. and Riemens, P. (2000) 'Amsterdam public digital culture'. Online at reinder.rustema.nl/dds/lovink/digitalculture2000.html (accessed 15 February 2005).
9. O'Leary, B. A., 20 April 1996. Personal communication.
10. Rheingold, H. (2000) *The Virtual Community: Homesteading on the Electronic Frontier.* Revised edition. Cambridge, MA: MIT Press.
11. Anfuso, D. (2004) 'That was then this is now', *iMedia Newsletter*, 25 February. Online at www.imediaconnection.com/content/2871.asp (accessed 15 February 2005).
12. Festa, P. (2000) 'Dot-com dead pool brakes for Ford', *C | Net News.com.* Online at news.com.com/2100-1023-955447.html (accessed 23 April 2005).
13. 'Bliz', 27 January 2005. Personal communication.
14. Travis, V., 10 January 2005. Personal communication.
15. Poore, J., 10 January 2005. Personal communication.
16. Nakamura, L. (2002) *Cybertypes: Race, Ethnicity, and Identity on the Internet.* New York: Routledge, p. 53.

9 From the margins to the mainstream

1. Law, L. (1982) *The Spectacle: A Skeleton Key* (Spectacular Times 8). London: Spectacular Times, p. 13.
2. Eden, D. (2004) 'Dissonance and mutations: theorising counter-culture', *Colloquy*, 8, May. Online at www.arts.monash.edu.au/others/colloquy/current/Eden.htm (accessed 23 April 2005).
3. James, M., 28 January 2005. Personal communication.
4. Elder, S. (2000) 'Village Voice sold', *Salon.com*, 4 January. Online at dir.salon.com/media/log/2000/01/04/voice/index.html (accessed 15 February 2005).
5. Redden, J., 28 January 2005. Personal communication
6. Brown, A. K. (2002) 'Who is your e-zine really FROM?' *EzineArticles.com*. Online at ezinearticles.com/?Who-Is-Your-E-zine-Really-FROM?&id=344 (accessed 15 February 2005).
7. Farhad, M. (2002) 'Flash: blogging goes corporate', *Wired News*, 9 May 2002. Online at www.wired.com/news/culture/0,1284,52380,00.html (accessed 15 February 2005).
8. Viguerie, R. A. (2004) *America's Right Turn: How Conservatives Used New and Alternative Media to Take Power*. Santa Monica, CA: Bonus Books.

10 New directions for a new century

1. Shah, A. (2001) 'WTO protests in Seattle'. Available at www.globalissues.org/TradeRelated/Seattle.asp (accessed 15 February 2005).
2. Roush, W. (2005) 'Larry Sanger's knowledge free-for-all', *TechnologyReview.com*, January. Online at www.technologyreview.com/articles/05/01/issue/forward30105.asp?trk=nl (accessed 15 February 2005).
3. Ilett, D. (2005) 'Vigilantes launch attack on scam sites', *C|Net News.com*, 10 February. Online at news.com.com/Vigilantes+launch+attack+on+scam+sites/2100-7349_3-5571061.html?tag=nefd.top (accessed 15 February 2005).
4. Clancy, H. (2005) 'Turning cellphones into scanners', *New York Times*, 12 February. Online at www.iht.com/articles/2005/02/11/business/ptphone12.html (accessed 15 February 2005).
5. Critical Art Ensemble (2005) 'Tactical projects'. Online at www.criticalart.net (accessed 15 February 2005).
6. Revolutionary Association of the Women of Afghanistan, 10 February 2005. Personal communication.
7. Gillmor, D. (2004) *We the Media: Grassroots Journalism By the People For the People*. Sebastopol, CA: O'Reilly.
8. Lasn, K. (2000) *Culture Jam: The Uncooling of America*. New York: HarperCollins, p. 185. Online at www.mediacarta.org (accessed 15 February 2005).

Bibliography

Abel, R. (1997) 'An alternative press: why?', *Publishing Research Quarterly*, 12 (4), pp. 78–84.

Ainley, B. (1998) *Black Journalists, White Media*. Stoke on Trent: Trentham Books.

Albert, Michael (2003) *ParEcon: Life After Capitalism*. London: Verso Books.

Alia, V. (2000) *Un/Covering the North: News, Media and Aboriginal People*. Vancouver, BC: University of British Columbia Press.

Atton, C. (1999) 'A reassessment of the alternative press', *Media, Culture & Society*, 21 (1), pp. 51–76.

Atton, C. (2002) *Alternative Media*. London: Sage.

Atton, C. (2005) *An Alternative Internet: Radical Media, Politics and Creativity*. Edinburgh: Edinburgh University Press.

Bagdikian, B. (2004) *The New Media Monopoly*. Boston: Beacon Press.

Barlow, W. (1998) *Voice Over: The Making of Black Radio*. Philadelphia: Temple University Press.

Barsamian, D. (2001) *The Decline and Fall of Public Broadcasting: Creating Alternative Media*. Cambridge, MA: South End Press.

Boyle, D. (1997) *Subject to Change: Guerrilla Television Revisited*. Oxford: Oxford University Press.

Branwyn, G. (1997) *Jamming the Media: A Citizen's Guide: Reclaiming the Tools of Communication*. San Francisco: Chronicle Books.

Brown, D. R. (1996) *Electronic Media and Indigenous Peoples: A Voice of Our Own?* Ames, IA: Iowa State University Press.

Carpenter, S. (2004) *40 Watts from Nowhere: A Journey into Pirate Radio*. New York: Scribner.

Center for Public Integrity (2000) *Citizen Muckraking: How to Investigate and Right Wrongs in Your Community*. Monroe, ME: Common Courage Press.

Chomsky, N. (2002) *Media Control: The Spectacular Achievements of Propaganda*. New York: Seven Stories Press.

Coleman, R. M. (ed.) (2002) *Say It Loud! African American Audiences, Media, and Identity*. New York: Garland.

Collin, M. (2002) *Guerrilla Radio: Rock'N'Roll Radio and Serbia's Underground Resistance*. New York: Nation Books.

Comedia (1984) 'The alternative press: the development of underdevelopment',

Media, Culture & Society, 6, pp. 95–102.

Couldry, N. and Curran, J. (2003) *Contesting Media Power: Alternative Media in a Networked World.* Totowa, NJ: Rowman & Littlefield.

Critical Art Ensemble (2001) *Digital Resistance: Explorations in Tactical Media.* New York: Autonomedia.

Critical Art Media (1996) *Electronic Civil Disobedience and Other Unpopular Ideas.* New York: Autonomedia.

Curran, J. and Gurevich, M. (eds) (2000) *Mass Media and Society.* London: Hodder Arnold.

Dana, R. (1986) *Against the Grain: Interviews with Maverick American Publishers.* Iowa City, IA: University of Iowa Press.

DeJong, W., Shaw, M., and Stammers, N. (2005) *Global Activism, Global Media.* London: Pluto Press.

Downing, J. (1980) *The Media Machine.* London: Pluto Press.

Downing, J. (2001) *Radical Media: Rebellious Communication and Social Movements.* Thousand Oaks, CA: Sage.

Downing, J., Mohammadi, A., and Sreberny, A. (eds) (1990) *Questioning the Media: A Critical Introduction.* Thousand Oaks, CA: Sage.

Draper, R. (1990) *Rolling Stone Magazine: The Uncensored History.* New York: Doubleday.

Duncombe, S. (1997) *Notes from Underground: Zines and the Politics of Alternative Culture.* London: Verso.

Dunifer, S. (2003) 'Seize the airwaves! Break the corporate media's stranglehold on the free flow of information, news, artistic expression and cultural creativity', *CounterPunch*, 24 July. Online at www.counterpunch.org/dunifer07252003.html (accessed 17 November 2004).

Farrelly, L. (2001) *Zines.* London: Booth-Clibborn Editions.

Fernandez, M., Wilding, F. and Wright, M. (2004) *Domain Errors! Cyberfeminist Practices.* London: Pluto Press.

Fortier, F. (2001) *Virtuality Check: Power Relations and Alternative Strategies in the Information Society.* London: Verso.

Fountain, N./Comedia (1988) *Underground: The London Alternative Press, 1966–74.* London: Routledge.

Frankfort, E. (1976) *The Voice: Life at the Village Voice.* New York: Morrow.

Fusco, M. and Hunt, I. (2004) *Put About: A Critical Anthology of Independent Publishing.* London: BookWorks.

Gillmor, D. (2004) *We the Media: Grassroots Journalism, By the People For the People.* Sebastopol, CA: O'Reilly.

Gitlin, T. (1980) *The Whole World is Watching: Mass Media and the Making and Unmaking of the New Left.* Berkeley, CA: University of California Press.

Goldberg, K. (1990) *The Barefoot Channel: Community Television as a Tool for Social Change.* Vancouver, BC: New Star.

Hackett, R. (2000) 'Taking back the media: notes on the potential for a communicative democracy movement', *Studies in Political Economy*, 63, pp. 61–86.

Halleck, D. (2002) *Hand-Held Visions: The Possibilities of Community Media.* Bronx,

NY: Fordham University Press.

Harding, T. (2001) *The Video Activist Handbook*. London: Pluto Press.

Hartley, J. and McKee, A. (2000) *The Indigenous Public Sphere: The Reporting and Reception of Indigenous Issues in the Australian Media 1994–1997*. Oxford: Oxford University Press.

Hazen, D. and Winokur, J. (eds) (1997) *We the Media: A Citizens' Guide to Fighting for Media Democracy*. New York: New Press.

Herman, E. S. and Chomsky, N. (1988) *Manufacturing Consent: The Political Economy of the Mass Media*. New York: Random House.

Iyengar, S. (1991) *Is Anyone Responsible? How Television Frames Political Issues*. Chicago: University of Chicago Press.

Jensen, R. (2002) *Writing Dissent: Taking Radical Ideas from the Margins to the Mainstream*. New York: Peter Lang.

Lasn, K. (2000) *Culture Jam: The Uncooling of America*. New York: HarperCollins.

Layne, K. (2003) 'The new underground newspaper', *Online Journalism Review*, 14 March. Online at www.ojr.org/ojr/business/1017961574.php (accessed 15 February 2005).

Lessig, L. (2004) *Free Culture: How Big Media Uses Technology and the Law to Lock Down Culture and Control Creativity*. New York: Penguin.

Levy, E. (2001) *Cinema of Outsiders: The Rise of American Independent Film*. New York: New York University Press.

McAuliffe, K. (1978) *The Great American Newspaper: The Rise and Fall of the Village Voice*. New York: Scribner and Sons.

McCaughey, M. and Ayers, M. D. (2003) *Cyberactivism: Online Activism in Theory and Practice*. New York: Routledge.

McChesney, R. (1997) *Corporate Media and the Threat to Democracy*. New York: Seven Stories Press.

McChesney, R. (1999) *Rich Media, Poor Democracy*. Champaign, IL: University of Illinois Press.

McChesney, R. (2004) *The Problem of the Media: US Communication Politics in the 21st Century*. New York: Monthly Review Press.

McChesney, R. and Nichols, J. (2002) *Our Media, Not Theirs: The Democratic Struggle Against Corporate Media*. New York: Seven Stories Press.

Murray, S. (2004) *Mixed Media: Feminist Presses and Publishing Politics*. London: Pluto Press.

Nakamura, L. (2002) *Cybertypes: Race, Ethnicity, and Identity on the Internet*. New York: Routledge.

Peck, A. (1985) *Uncovering the Sixties: The Life and Times of the Underground Press*. New York: Pantheon Books.

Phillips, P. (ed.) (2003) *Project Censored Guide to Independent Media and Activism*. New York: Seven Stories Press.

Pierson, J. (1996) *Spike, Mike, Slackers and Dykes: A Guided Tour Across a Decade of American Independent Cinema*. New York: Hyperion.

Rodríguez, C. (2001) *Fissures in the Mediascape: An International Study of Citizens' Media*. Cresskill, NJ: Hampton Press.

Ross, K. and Byerly, C. M. (2004) *Women and Media: International Perspectives.* Oxford: Blackwell.

Rowe, C. (1997) *The Book of Zines: Readings from the Fringe.* New York: Owl Books.

Ruggiero, G. and Olshansky, B. (1999) *Microradio and Democracy: (Low) Power to the People.* New York: Seven Stories Press.

Ryan, C. (1991) *Prime-Time Activism: Media Strategies for Grass-Roots Organizing.* Boston: South End Press.

Sakolsky, R. and Dunifer, S. (eds) (1998) *Seizing the Airwaves: A Free Radio Handbook.* Edinburgh: AK Press.

Salzman, J. (2003) *Making the News: A Guide for Activists and Nonprofits.* Boulder, CO: Westview Press.

Skilling, H. G. (1989) *Samizdat and an Independent Society in Central and Eastern Europe.* Columbus, OH: Ohio State University Press.

Strauss, N. and Mandl, D. (1996) *Radiotext(e).* New York: Semiotext(e).

Switzer, L. and Adhikari, M. (eds) (2000) *South Africa's Resistance Press: Alternative Voices in the Last Generation Under Apartheid.* Columbus, OH: Ohio University Press.

Thompson, N. and Sholette, G. (eds) (2004) *The Interventionists: Users' Manual for the Creative Disruption of Everyday Life.* Cambridge, MA: MIT Press.

Trippi, J. (2004) *The Revolution Will Not Be Televised: Democracy, the Internet, and the Overthrow of Everything.* New York: Regan Books.

Turkle, S. (1997) *Life on the Screen: Identity in the Age of the Internet.* New York: Simon & Schuster.

Vale, V. (1999) *Zines! Vol. 1: Interviews With Independent Publishers.* San Francisco: V/Search.

Wakefield, S. and Grrrt (2003) *Not for Rent: Conversations With Creative Activists in the UK.* Second edition. New York: Evil Twin Publications.

Walker, J. (2004) *Rebels on the Air: An Alternative History of Radio in America.* New York: New York University Press.

Waschsberger, K. (ed.) (1993) *Voices from the Underground: Insider Histories of the Vietnam Era Underground Press,* vols 1 and 2. Tempe, AZ: MICA Press.

Wayne, M. (1998) *Dissident Voices: The Politics of Television and Cultural Change.* London: Pluto Press.

Internet resources

Adbusters magazine: adbusters.org/home
Alliance for Community Media: www.alliancecm.org
Alternative Media Watch: www.zmag.org/altmediawatch.htm
Alternative Press Center/Independent Press Association: www.altpress.org
Alternative Press Review: www.altpr.org
AltWeeklies.com: www.altweeklies.com
Association of Alternative Newsweeklies: aan.org/gyrobase/Aan/index
Association of Independent Video and Filmmakers: www.aivf.org
Clandestine Radio: www.clandestineradio.com
Communication Rights in the Information Society (CRIS): www.crisinfo.org
Community Media Association: www.commedia.org.uk
DIY Media: www.diymedia.net
The E-zine List: www.e-zine-list.com
Free Press: www.freepress.net
Grassroots Radio Coalition: www.kgnu.org/grassroots
Grrl Zine Network: grrrlzines.net
Guerrilla News Network: www.guerrillanews.com
Independent Media Centres: www.indymedia.org
Independent Press Association: www.indypress.org
Media Access Project: www.mediaaccess.org
National Alliance for Media Arts and Culture (NAMAC): www.namac.org
NewPages: Alternatives in Print & Media: www.newpages.com
OURMedia/NUESTROSMedias: www.ourmedianet.org
Prometheus Radio Project: www.prometheusradio.org
Radio4All: www.radio4all.org

Index